D0782863

AIDS in South Asia

AIDS in South Asia

Understanding and Responding to a Heterogeneous Epidemic

Stephen Moses
James F. Blanchard
Han Kang
Faran Emmanuel
Sushena Reza Paul
Marissa L. Becker
David Wilson
Mariam Claeson

THE WORLD BANK
Washington, DC

©2006 The International Bank for Reconstruction and Development / The World Bank
1818 H Street NW
Washington DC 20433
Telephone: 202-473-1000
Internet: www.worldbank.org
E-mail: feedback@worldbank.org

All rights reserved

1 2 3 4 09 08 07 06

This volume is a product of the staff of the International Bank for Reconstruction and Development / The World Bank. The findings, interpretations, and conclusions expressed in this volume do not necessarily reflect the views of the Executive Directors of The World Bank or the governments they represent.

The World Bank does not guarantee the accuracy of the data included in this work. The boundaries, colors, denominations, and other information shown on any map in this work do not imply any judgement on the part of The World Bank concerning the legal status of any territory or the endorsement or acceptance of such boundaries.

Rights and Permissions
The material in this publication is copyrighted. Copying and/or transmitting portions or all of this work without permission may be a violation of applicable law. The International Bank for Reconstruction and Development / The World Bank encourages dissemination of its work and will normally grant permission to reproduce portions of the work promptly.

For permission to photocopy or reprint any part of this work, please send a request with complete information to the Copyright Clearance Center Inc., 222 Rosewood Drive, Danvers, MA 01923, USA; telephone: 978-750-8400; fax: 978-750-4470; Internet: www.copyright.com.

All other queries on rights and licenses, including subsidiary rights, should be addressed to the Office of the Publisher, The World Bank, 1818 H Street NW, Washington, DC 20433, USA; fax: 202-522-2422; e-mail: pubrights@worldbank.org.

ISBN-10: 0-8213-6757-9
ISBN-13: 978-0-8213-6757-5
eISBN: 0-8213-6758-7
DOI: 10.1596/978-0-8213-6757-5

Library of Congress Cataloging-in-Publications Data has been requested.

Contents

Figures, Tables, and Boxes

Figures

Tables

Boxes

Foreword

South Asia is facing a severe HIV epidemic in magnitude and scope, with an estimated 5.5 million to 6 million people infected. At least 60 percent of HIV-positive people in Asia live in India alone. The epidemic is not homogenous and requires well informed, prioritized, and effective responses. This report attempts to provide the basis for rigorous, evidence-informed HIV policy and programming and to increase understanding of the diversity of the epidemic between and within the countries of the South Asia Region.

A diverse range of structural factors amplify HIV vulnerability and risk in the region, including widespread poverty and socioeconomic inequality, illiteracy, low social status of women, trafficking of women into commercial sex, and a large sex work industry. The region's borders are porous, permitting widespread rural-urban, interstate, and international migration. High rates of sexually transmitted infections and limited condom use prevail, and social stigma is an important impediment to delivering effective programs.

This report describes how sex work and injecting drug use fuel concentrated epidemics. Men who have sex with men represent an important vulnerable population, but more information is required to better understand their role in HIV transmission dynamics. The report also draws attention to significant rural epidemics in parts of India and Nepal and the need to increase understanding of HIV prevention needs and service delivery patterns in South Asia's rural settings. Understanding rural epidemics and configuring an effective response to them constitute a major challenge.

The report argues for an effective two-pronged approach:

- first, and foremost, scaling up effective HIV prevention programs for high-risk vulnerable groups; and

- second, tackling the underlying socioeconomic determinants of the epidemic.

The latter include stigma and discrimination toward marginalized people engaging in high-risk behaviors and people living with HIV/AIDS.

The report's authors benefited from the contribution of many partners, both in the country-by-country analyses and in the review process. A series of consultations triggered a lively discussion of how to use a better understanding of the epidemic to develop a stronger response. Despite the severity of the epidemic, it can still be contained, and we hope that the report will stimulate discussion and inform strong and effective policies and programs to combat the AIDS epidemic in South Asia.

Julian Schweitzer
Director
Human Development Department
South Asia Region

Debrework Zewdie
Director
Global HIV/AIDS Program

Acknowledgments

We would like to thank all who contributed to the review of this report, including the peer reviewers: Olusoji Adeyi, Tim Brown, and Susan Stout. Denis Broun, Shanti Conoly, Ruben del Prado, Ted Karpf, DCS Reddy, Neff Walker, and Anandi Yuvaraj participated as discussants in a series of country, regional and international consultations to review the report and discuss its preliminary findings. We would also like to thank the World Bank HIV/AIDS country office teams in Bangladesh, India, Nepal, Pakistan, and Sri Lanka who helped in shaping the messages, including Sundar Gopalan, Shirin Jahangeer, Kees Kostermans, Kumari Navaratne, Tirtha Rana, and Suneeta Singh, and many others who provided useful critiques of the draft report.

The task was co-managed by the World Bank South Asia Regional AIDS team, including Hnin Hnin Pyne, Sandra Rosenhouse, and Mariam Claeson under the direction of Julian Schweitzer and Anabela Abreu, and David Wilson of the World Bank's Global HIV/AIDS Program, under the direction of Debrework Zewdie. It was a collaborative effort of the World Bank and the University of Manitoba. Stephen Moses, James Blanchard, Han Kang, David Wilson, Faran Emmanuel, Sushena Reza Paul, Marissa Becker, and Mariam Claeson coauthored the report.

We thank Phoebe Folger for her assistance and Paola Scalabrin and others from the Office of the Publisher for their editorial assistance.

Finally, the team gratefully acknowledges the generous support of the Government of the Netherlands through the Bank-Netherlands Partnership Program.

Abbreviations

AIDS	Acquired immune deficiency syndrome
ANC	Antenatal clinic
AusAID	Australian Agency for International Development
BSS	Behavioral surveillance survey
CIDA	Canadian International Development Agency
DfID	Department for International Development (United Kingdom)
FHI	Family Health International
FSW	Female sex worker
HIV	Human immunodeficiency virus
IBBS	Integrated biological and behavioral surveillance
ICDDRB	International Centre for Diarrhoeal Disease Research, Bangladesh
IDU	Injecting drug use(r)
IEC	Information, education, and communication
M&E	Monitoring and evaluation
MOH	Ministry of Health
MOHFW	Ministry of Health and Family Welfare (Bangladesh and India)
MSM	Men having sex with men
MTP	Medium-term plan
NAC	National AIDS Committee (Bangladesh and Sri Lanka) or National AIDS Council (Nepal)
NACC	National AIDS Coordination Committee (Nepal)
NACO	National AIDS Control Organization (India)

NACP	National AIDS Control Program (the agenda of HIV/AIDS activities in India and Nepal, as well as the federal government HIV/AIDS agency in Pakistan)
NASP	National AIDS and STD Program (Bangladesh)
NCASC	National Centre for AIDS and STD Control (Nepal)
NGO	Nongovernmental organization
NSACP	National STD and AIDS Control Program (Sri Lanka)
NWFP	Northwest Frontier Province (Pakistan)
PACP	Provincial AIDS Control Program (Pakistan)
PLWHA	People living with HIV/AIDS
RTI	Reproductive tract infection
SACS	State AIDS Control and Prevention Societies (India)
SAR	South Asia region
STI	Sexually transmitted infection
SW	Sex work(er)
TB	Tuberculosis
UN	United Nations
UNAIDS	The Joint United Nations Programme on HIV/AIDS
UNDP	United Nations Development Programme
UNFPA	United Nations Fund for Population Activities
UNICEF	United Nations Children's Education Fund
UNODC	United Nations Office on Drug Control and Crime
USAID	United States Agency for International Development
VCT	Voluntary counseling and testing
WHO	World Health Organization

Executive Summary

South Asia's HIV epidemic is severe in magnitude and scope, with at least 60 percent of all people with HIV in Asia living in India. Because the HIV epidemic is highly heterogeneous, designing informed, prioritized, and effective responses necessitates an understanding of the epidemic's diversity between and within countries. This review was undertaken to provide a basis for rigorous, evidence-based HIV policy and programming in South Asia.

Focus

This book focuses on five South Asian countries for which significant data are available:

- Bangladesh

- India

- Nepal

- Pakistan

- Sri Lanka.

Although data limitations preclude detailed analyses for Afghanistan, Bhutan, and the Maldives, data from those countries are cited where available. The monograph focuses on prevention, but it also acknowledges and affirms the important and complementary role of treatment.

Heterogeneity

South Asia is a heterogeneous and highly mobile region. South Asia's most severe epidemics occur in parts of India, particularly in a cluster of southern and western states, including Tamil Nadu, Karnataka, Andhra Pradesh, Goa, and Maharashtra, where sex work is the critical driver of HIV transmission. Epidemics also occur in some northeastern states, including Mizoram, Nagaland, and Manipur, where injecting drug use is a major driver of transmission. In these states, HIV prevalence varies between districts; between subdistricts (variously called blocks, *tahsils*, or *talukas*); and even between villages in the same block. The HIV epidemic may be as severe in parts of Nepal, where transmission occurs largely through sex work and injecting drug use, and among the sexual partners of those engaging in injecting drug use. Both Bangladesh and Pakistan face growing epidemics, particularly among injecting drug users (IDUs), but HIV rates remain relatively low among sex workers (SWs) in those countries, providing an opportunity to avert a major heterosexual epidemic. HIV prevalence in Sri Lanka remains low, even among vulnerable groups. In all of these countries, men having sex with men (MSM) represent an important vulnerable population, but much more information is required to better understand their role in the dynamics of HIV transmission. Despite Afghanistan's limited HIV data, the country must act urgently to curb rapidly growing HIV infection in its large population of IDUs, especially where drug use and the sex trade intersect. Other South Asian countries—Bhutan and the Maldives—have too little data to form a core focus of this review, but data are adequate to suggest that they still have low-prevalence epidemics.

Structural Amplifiers

All countries in South Asia have a diverse range of structural factors that amplify HIV vulnerability and risk, including widespread poverty and inequality; illiteracy; low social status of women; trafficking of women into commercial sex; a large, structured sex work industry; porous borders; widespread rural-urban, interstate, and international migration; high levels of mobility; stigma and cultural impediments to sexual discussion; high rates of sexually transmitted infections (STIs); and limited condom use.

A Preventable Epidemic

South Asia's HIV epidemic is severe, but further spread is preventable. The future size of South Asia's epidemic will depend on an effective two-pronged approach. First, and most critical, the epidemic's growth will depend on the scope and effectiveness of HIV prevention programs for male and female SWs and their clients, for IDUs and their sexual partners, and for MSM and their sexual partners. Second, it will depend on the effectiveness of efforts to address the underlying socioeconomic determinants of the epidemic and to reduce stigma and discrimination toward people engaging in high-risk behaviors, who are often the marginalized in society, as well as toward people living with HIV/AIDS.

Success of Prevention Efforts

HIV prevention programs for SWs, IDUs, and MSM in South Asia have worked to a large extent. Results have been achieved through targeted interventions aimed at reducing risk behaviors and exposure. Furthermore, countries such as India are making strides in tackling stigma and discrimination, although much remains to be done. The AIDS community is gaining experience on how to work through key sectors other than health, such as the transportation sector, to effectively reach potential clients of SWs. Achieving high coverage poses the greatest challenge today: reducing HIV transmission requires saturation of preventive interventions among people engaged in high-risk behaviors.

Prevention Programs' Cost-Effectiveness

HIV prevention among SWs and clients, IDUs and their sexual partners, and MSM and their sexual partners is relatively inexpensive and provides a high return on investment. Effective programs for SWs, IDUs, MSM, and sexual partners of these individuals can reduce their HIV risk and prevent further viral spread. Such actions will greatly reduce the costs of controlling HIV infection and will mitigate the socioeconomic impact. HIV programs' priorities and investments should closely address these transmission patterns and their key structural determinants.

Rural Epidemics

Evidence is growing of significant rural epidemics in parts of India and Nepal, but knowledge is lacking of HIV prevention needs and service delivery patterns in South Asia's rural settings. Understanding rural epidemics and configuring an effective response to them constitute a major challenge.

Country Priorities

Each country faces its own challenges and has to set its own priorities.

India

The future size of India's HIV epidemic will depend above all on the scope and effectiveness of programs for SWs and clients; however, it also will depend on the scope and effectiveness of programs for MSM and their other sexual partners, and IDUs and their sexual partners, the latter particularly in the northeast. Throughout India, tackling stigma and discrimination toward people engaging in high-risk behaviors and those living with HIV remains vital. In certain high-prevalence states, districts, and subdistricts (blocks, *tahsils*, and *talukas*), tailoring and applying focused strategies to reduce HIV transmission into vulnerable segments of the general population also constitute a programmatic priority. HIV prevention and HIV/AIDS treatment have potential reciprocal benefits: HIV prevention makes treatment more affordable, and treatment creates important opportunities for enhanced HIV prevention.

Nepal

The future size of Nepal's HIV epidemic will depend above all on the scope and effectiveness of programs for SWs and clients, as well as for

IDUs and their sexual partners. Cross-border migration, especially involving women migrating or being trafficked into sex work, particularly to Mumbai, increases HIV transmission. The national response should also address the further risk of sex between men. Nepal's continuing internal civil strife poses a formidable challenge but also increases the importance of civil society's contributions to the country's response. Tackling stigma and discrimination is a priority, as elsewhere in the region, and efforts to reduce trafficking of women are critical.

Pakistan and Bangladesh

The current HIV epidemics in both Pakistan and Bangladesh occur mainly within networks of IDUs, with evidence of limited but growing epidemic spread among MSM and *hijras* (transgendered men). Effective prevention programs among those communities may avert a wider epidemic. The possible spread of HIV from IDUs to networks of male and female SWs will increase the severity of the epidemic and narrow a major window of opportunity for prevention. In Bangladesh in particular, levels of risk are high, exacerbated by mobility and individuals' rapid transition from smoking drugs to injecting drugs. The potential therefore exists for a substantial epidemic if significant spread occurs among IDU networks, and particularly if these networks intersect with commercial sex networks. HIV infection among SWs in both countries remains at a low level, and intensive programs for them and their clients—including a major focus on SWs who inject drugs or whose sexual partners inject drugs—can prevent the epidemics from escalating. High-quality programs with wide coverage necessitate a reduction in stigma for those groups.

Sri Lanka

The HIV epidemic remains at a low level in Sri Lanka, even among high-risk groups. Early and effective programs for SWs and their clients, and for MSM and their other sexual partners, can ensure that HIV remains at very low levels if those programs are combined with programs to detect any growth in injection drug use and to increase capacity to manage opiate addiction. Sri Lanka has an opportunity that it must not lose.

Afghanistan

The evidence suggests considerable HIV transmission among some of Afghanistan's IDUs. IDUs returning from Iran, which has a significant injecting drug use epidemic, are at high risk. The country must act urgently to limit HIV infection in this high-risk subpopulation.

Bhutan and the Maldives

Data are limited; however, these disparate countries—for very different reasons—appear to have low HIV prevalence and relatively small numbers of IDUs, SWs, and clients. Nevertheless, recent observational accounts suggest that injecting drug use may be growing in the Maldives.

Programmatic Implications and Conclusion

South Asia requires a dual approach to HIV prevention. Most important is to have effective large-scale programs for SWs and clients, IDUs and their sexual partners, and MSM and their sexual partners. Second, support for these programs must include information on HIV prevention for the general population and stigma reduction in particular. Capable and committed individuals and groups are needed to facilitate program implementation at all administrative levels. Given the enormous scale and heterogeneity of the HIV epidemic in South Asia, governments and their program implementing partners need to invest in building and using a comprehensive information base to identify the priority constituents and locations for focused prevention programs. In addition, improving the scale, coverage, quality, and integrity of program implementation requires substantial capacity building. Multisectoral responses can address both the immediate practices and the underlying socioeconomic factors that contribute to transmission. Large-scale, targeted prevention programs with saturation coverage based on these principles can greatly decrease the size of South Asia's HIV epidemic, prevent the establishment of an epidemic in the general population, markedly reduce expenditures for disease control, and mitigate socioeconomic impact, hence providing a high return on investment.

CHAPTER 1

Background and Rationale

The countries of the South Asia Region of the World Bank are Afghanistan, Bangladesh, Bhutan, India, the Maldives, Nepal, Pakistan, and Sri Lanka. As a large and diverse region, it has a complex, heterogeneous HIV epidemic, with considerable variation within and between countries. The first set of AIDS cases appeared in the region during the early 1980s, and by the end of the decade, national health authorities of most countries had received reports of AIDS cases. Despite similar times of HIV introduction, the epidemics in the various countries have played out in remarkably different ways. Indeed, this divergence has occurred even within individual countries. India could even be considered a continent in itself, with individual states or even smaller geographic units with unique epidemic patterns that require different responses. Indeed, a major lesson from Africa—a continent with approximately half the population of India—is the need to understand the remarkable diversity. This lesson has received insufficient emphasis in South Asia and globally.

This book is based on surveillance and other relevant information to date, both published and unpublished. It focuses on five countries in the region for which adequate secondary data from these sources exist to synthesize a regional analysis: Bangladesh, India, Nepal, Pakistan, and Sri Lanka. Brief comments are also offered on the HIV epidemics in Afghanistan, Bhutan, and the Maldives, but information is not sufficient to support an in-depth analysis.

Throughout this report "high-risk group" refers to a group or community of people engaging in practices or behaviors that put them at increased risk for HIV acquisition and transmission.

1

Rationale

Rigorous analysis should inform the policies and programs needed to curb the region's complex and diverse HIV epidemic. In particular, this analysis should entail an understanding of HIV epidemiology, HIV transmission dynamics and the behavioral and socioeconomic determinants of the epidemic, its potential evolution, response priorities, and gaps.

In the third decade of the global HIV epidemic, the world health community has a greater understanding of the global distribution of HIV as well as of the biobehavioral determinants and underlying contextual and structural factors of HIV transmission. Such understanding can inform an appropriate HIV prevention and control response. To date, however, generic approaches have failed to address the major epidemic drivers in local contexts, undermining HIV programs in some countries. Informed approaches would encompass prioritized and tailored activities for a more effective response. In Nepal, for example, over 30 percent of the budget of the National Centre for AIDS and Sexually Transmitted Disease Control has been spent on general population interventions, and only 6 percent has been spent on harm reduction programs for injecting drug users (IDUs), although drug use is a major driver of the HIV epidemic (FHI and NCASC 2002). In India, more targeted interventions managed by nongovernmental organizations (NGOs) have been funded for migrant men than for female sex workers (SWs), even though the latter group is much more central to HIV transmission dynamics. Alongside an understanding of transmission dynamics and priority responses, we have learned the mechanics of configuring and carrying out such responses. Implementation should occur on a large scale and reach a majority of those people at risk of infection, exemplifying the time-honored public health mantra to "do the right thing, do it right, and do enough of it."

Nowhere are these principles more important than in Asia, whose size, complexities, and disparities within and between countries compel an intelligent epidemiological analysis and effective, focused responses. Despite the diversity of Asia's HIV epidemic, sufficient commonalities characterize broad continental epidemic patterns.

What are the central features of the Asian HIV epidemic? In Asia, high-risk behaviors drive much of the epidemic: injecting drug use and unprotected commercial sex, plus anal sex among subsets of the population. The sexual partners of those engaging in these behaviors also have an elevated risk of acquiring and transmitting HIV. The overall size of the Asian epidemic therefore depends on several characteristics of these networks, such as the prevalence of HIV, number of sexual or IDU partners, extent of their risk behaviors, interaction with the wider community, and extent of preventive measures. In some Asian countries, such as Cambodia, Thailand, and much of India, the scale and frequency of commercial sex have surpassed a critical point to ignite sexual epidemics among SWs, their clients, and a growing number of sexual partners of such clients. In other countries, such as China, Indonesia, and Vietnam, injecting drug use has initiated epidemics that have spread to SWs and then to their clients and beyond. Throughout Asia, unprotected anal intercourse, predominantly between men, constitutes a significant source of HIV transmission and warrants further study. In sum, HIV spreads among high-risk groups to their immediate sexual partners and then into the wider community, presenting a major development challenge.

These patterns highlight the need for large-scale and well-covered interventions that are informed by an elucidation of two behavioral determinants of transmission:

- sexual contact

- injecting drug use.

A complementary analysis and understanding of socioeconomic determinants will also contribute to intervention design. South Asia is characterized by poverty, inequality, gender inequity, migration, human trafficking, and proximity to the "golden crescent"—the nerve center of the global opium trade—all of which can mediate the behavioral determinants of HIV transmission.

The concepts of HIV risk and vulnerability are frequently referenced in this book. Individuals or groups may be at higher risk for HIV than the general population for either behavioral or biological reasons, or for both. Although everyone is potentially at risk for acquiring HIV infection, key subpopulations such as SWs, their clients, men who have sex with men, and IDUs are at higher risk than others, and if they are infected, they are more likely to transmit infection to large numbers of partners or contacts. The level of HIV risk for such subpopulations, however, is highly influenced by broader extrinsic factors that increase their vulnerability by impeding their ability to adopt and practice safer sexual behaviors. For example, vulnerability factors for rural female SWs in India could include early age of initiation of sex work, geographic mobility, low levels of literacy, and low education levels in rural communities. A clear understanding of both risk and vulnerability is required to effectively implement programs to prevent HIV transmission.

As suggested by the broad continental epidemic patterns, much of the literature on HIV in Asia stems from the evidence and experiences of East Asian countries. More recently, that literature has encompassed a growing body of biological and behavioral studies in South Asia that provide the basis for a better understanding of epidemic patterns specific to the region, but few of those studies have been analyzed and interpreted in an integrated, systematic manner. This gap calls for a rigorous analysis and synthesis of the major biobehavioral determinants and trends in South Asia's HIV epidemic, which should be reinforced by an equally rigorous review of the evidence base, scope, and reach for various existing interventions across and within South Asian countries. To underscore the importance of intracountry analyses, one might consider that the notion of a national epidemic in a country as vast and diverse as India—let alone the wider South Asian region—belies the reality of multiple, variegated local epidemics.

This book undertakes such an analysis in South Asia to fulfill the following objectives:

- provide a state-of-the-art assessment of South Asia's existing HIV epidemic, its major transmission dynamics, and its potential evolution

- propose a rigorous, evidence-based, practical HIV response strategy for the region

- highlight priorities for greater emphasis in South Asia's HIV responses.

We also hope that this analysis will stimulate a discussion about priorities, strategic focus, and resource allocation among all partners involved in mounting an effective response to curb the HIV epidemic in South Asia by 2015:

- governments
- bilateral and multilateral agencies
- nongovernmental organizations
- the private sector
- other civil society groups.

CHAPTER 2

Analytic Framework

Between and within South Asian countries, the diversity of biological, behavioral, and structural factors can explain the substantial heterogeneity in HIV epidemiology and transmission dynamics (MAP 2005). Formulating strategies to curb the region's HIV epidemic necessitates a comprehensive understanding of this diversity. Despite the large gaps in data and information necessary to complete this task thoroughly, we believe that an analysis of the extant data is sufficient to provide broad strategic guidance. We have developed a descriptive and anticipatory analytic approach that is based on two epidemiological concepts: *epidemic potential* and *epidemic phase*.

Epidemic Potential

Largely on the basis of an analysis of the size and distribution of key high-risk subpopulations (for example, sex workers, or SWs, and clients of sex workers; injecting drug users, or IDUs; and men having sex with men, or MSM), as well as the nature of sexual networking, an assessment of the *epidemic potential* focuses primarily on the extent of maintaining and amplifying an HIV epidemic beyond the spread within networks that are directly linked to high-risk subpopulations. For this analysis, we consider three types of epidemics, which are based on potential:

- truncated

- local concentrated

- generalizing epidemics.

Truncated Epidemic

The term *truncated epidemic* describes a situation of HIV transmission that is confined to individuals who participate in nonlocalized high-risk networks, such as commercial sex or IDU-sharing networks, and to their local partners. *Localization* is defined with reference to the origin, typically a place of residence that is connected to those networks through bridge populations. An example is provided by a rural area with a substantial number of out-migrants who travel to an urban migration destination to work, and who engage in commercial sex while there but who do not engage in high-risk behaviors to the same extent in their rural homes. In this circumstance, transmission may occur among the sexual partners of returning migrants without further amplification by local high-risk networks of transmission. Accordingly, prevention strategies should focus primarily on interrupting transmission at the migration destination points, with prevention message reinforcement at the origin and transit points in areas that have very large concentrations of out-migrants. Service delivery at the locations of origin should emphasize HIV counseling and testing services targeted especially to individuals with high-risk behavior, as well as care and support services. Figure 2.1 schematically depicts a truncated epidemic.

As we discuss later in this document, truncated epidemics are likely in many rural locations of Pakistan and India, where the local sexual structure does not support much local HIV transmission, but where a significant proportion of men out-migrate to urban areas with large commercial sex networks. Those men may acquire HIV infection after engaging in high-risk behaviors as part of the networks at their

Figure 2.1 Truncated Epidemic

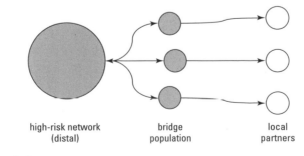

high-risk network	bridge	local
(distal)	population	partners

Source: Authors.

migration destination and then may infect their sexual partners without spreading HIV beyond the partner.

Local Concentrated Epidemic

The term *local concentrated epidemic* refers to an epidemic characterized by substantially enough spread networks locally (such as SW or IDU networks) to initiate and sustain local transmission within high-risk subpopulations and to the wider local population through bridge populations. The size of the high-risk subpopulations and other sexual networks in the local area would largely determine the size of such epidemics, but HIV transmission dynamics remain driven by the high-risk networks. Prevention strategies in this type of epidemic would need to focus on interrupting transmission within both the distal and the local high-risk transmission networks. Schematically, figure 2.2 depicts a local concentrated epidemic.

This epidemic pattern is the most important one in South Asia; it is epitomized by the many locations with substantial high-risk sexual and IDU networks. Although HIV prevalence within those networks reaches high levels, the prevalence in the general population will not reach levels much beyond 1 to 3 percent unless a very high proportion of men (perhaps 20 percent) are clients of sex workers (NCHADS 2002). This constraint on overall epidemic growth occurs because of

Figure 2.2 Local Concentrated Epidemic

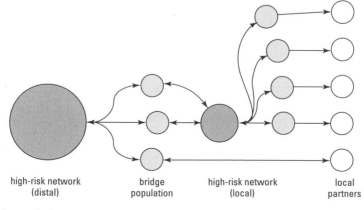

high-risk network (distal)　　　bridge population　　　high-risk network (local)　　　local partners

Source: Authors.

limited transmission between local partners who are independent of high-risk networks.

Generalizing Epidemic

Generalizing epidemics begin in local high-risk networks, but because of extensive risk behaviors in the wider community, the HIV epidemic spreads beyond the highest-risk networks. Ultimately, transmission occurs somewhat independent of easily defined high-risk groups. Strategic responses to such situations should include both targeted interventions for high-risk groups and an early emphasis on reducing the potential for transmission in the more general population through enhanced sexually transmitted infection (STI) services, broader behavioral change programs, and aggressive condom promotion. Figure 2.3 schematically depicts a generalizing epidemic.

Generalizing epidemics occur in many countries of Sub-Saharan Africa, but as we discuss subsequently, many locations in South Asia do not exhibit the defining conditions—such as substantial transmission beyond the high-risk networks—to sustain and amplify this kind of epidemic. Possible exceptions may include some localized areas in southern India, particularly in the states of Andhra Pradesh, Karnataka, and Maharashtra, as well as in parts of northeast India, particularly in the states of Manipur, Mizoram, and Nagaland.

Although concentrated and generalizing epidemics will generally result in higher HIV prevalence, this measure does not strictly define those typologies. Instead, the transmission structure in terms of

Figure 2.3 Generalizing Epidemic

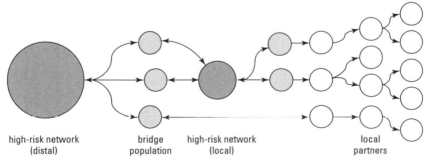

| high-risk network | bridge | high-risk network | local |
| (distal) | population | (local) | partners |

Source: Authors.

behavioral patterns and networks constitutes a distinguishing character-
istic. Indeed, local concentrated epidemics could result in having HIV
prevalence in the general adult population exceed 1 percent (as, for
example, in districts in Manipur) if the sizes of high-risk subpopulations
are large enough. On the one hand, an epidemic is concentrated if it is
driven primarily by high-risk groups and if effective programs for high-
risk groups would reduce overall HIV transmission. On the other hand,
an epidemic is generalized if transmission occurs primarily outside high-
risk groups and would continue despite effective programs for high-risk
groups. In short, an epidemic is concentrated if stopping high-risk group
transmission would control the epidemic, and it is generalized if stopping high-risk group transmission would not control the epidemic.

Epidemic Phase

Conceptually, the *epidemic phase* describes the extent to which an HIV
epidemic has progressed along its expected trajectory in terms of its
subpopulation distribution, which is determined by the epidemic potential described in the preceding section. Solely on the basis of HIV
prevalence, an early-phase generalizing epidemic will not appear to be
much different from a later-phase concentrated epidemic. An assessment of the epidemic phase serves as a diagnostic tool, but the challenge
lies not only in measuring HIV prevalence in different subpopulations
and in understanding when HIV was introduced into the populations,
but also in understanding the HIV-associated risk in subpopulations
(especially to SWs and clients) and the factors related to sexual and nee-
dle-sharing networks. Each type of epidemic can occur at an "incipi-
ent," "growth," "plateau," or "decline" phase as depicted in figure 2.4.

Biological Factors

Biological factors related to the virus or population can mitigate the
spread of HIV infection. A detailed discussion of those factors—many of
which remain inadequately understood—is beyond the scope of this
book, but the most important factor that does appear to influence the pattern of HIV spread in South Asia is male circumcision. The following

Figure 2.4 Phases of an Epidemic

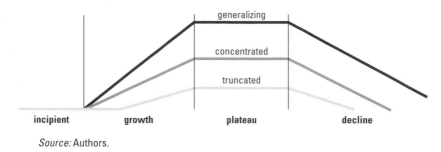

Source: Authors.

comments are not intended as an argument for male circumcision as a recommended public health intervention in South Asia, but as a heuristic approach to understanding the epidemic potential in the region. Scientists have noted an association between male circumcision and HIV rates since the 1980s (Bongaarts and others 1989), including in India (Reynolds and others 2004). The biological basis for this relationship is plausible (Patterson and others 2002; Szabo and Short 2000), and a meta-analysis of 38 studies from Africa has concluded that uncircumcised men were more than twice as likely to have HIV as circumcised men (Weiss, Quigley, and Hayes 2000). In mid-2005, a randomized trial comparing circumcised and uncircumcised men in Orange Farm, South Africa, demonstrated a protective effect of about 60 percent (Auvert and others 2005).

As a summary of the implications for South Asia, male circumcision is widespread in Afghanistan, Bangladesh, and Pakistan. Therefore, a more limited potential for heterosexual HIV epidemics is likely in those countries. However, injecting drug use may ignite otherwise dormant epidemics, particularly if a nexus between injecting drug use and sex work exists in those countries. HIV transmission among MSM may also play a proportionately greater role in Afghanistan, Bangladesh, and Pakistan, primarily because of greater transmission efficiency related to anal intercourse. Conversely, the absence of extensive male circumcision may increase the relative epidemic potential in other South Asian countries, particularly where circumcision coincides with other behavioral and structural factors, as discussed next. In conclusion, male circumcision is one factor explaining the epidemic dynamics of the region.

The analysis in this report focuses mainly on the sexual transmission of HIV infection and transmission through injection drug use. HIV transmission through transfusion of infected blood or blood products may still occur to a limited degree, but in all national programs in the region, blood safety has been a priority since early in the HIV epidemic. Little evidence exists that significant transmission of HIV now occurs through this route. Similarly, little evidence exists of HIV transmission through unsafe medical injections. However, medical injections are extremely common in the region (Lakshman and Nichter 2000), and population-based longitudinal studies are required—using detailed and accurate measures of parenteral exposures—to accurately assess their relationships with risk for HIV infection in those settings (Becker and others 2005).

Behavioral and Structural Factors

In addition to biological factors, behavioral and structural factors influence epidemic potential. A robust association between the number of sexual partners or rate of partner change and the likelihood of sexual HIV transmission appears in many contexts. Another factor—patterns of partner change—can affect this probability (Halperin and Epstein 2004), given the potential of exposure to a partner with acute HIV infection. Growing biological evidence suggests that the HIV viral load and, thus, the infectivity are far higher during acute HIV infection—that is, in the initial weeks after HIV infection (Chao and others 1994; Quinn and others 2000)—thereby leading to the important distinction between serial and concurrent patterns of sexual partnerships in terms of HIV risk (Halperin and Epstein 2004).

In serial partnerships, an individual typically has one ongoing sexual relationship at a time. In concurrent partnerships, one may participate in a sexual network with more than one ongoing sexual relationship at a time. Whereas serial partnerships limit exposure to one partner with acute HIV infection (the partner who has higher infectivity), concurrent partnerships expose all participants in an ongoing sexual network of greater risk. Mathematical models suggest that concurrent sexual partnerships may increase HIV transmission tenfold. Growing biological evidence of variability in viral load and infectivity firmly supports those projections (Morris and Kretzschmar 1997). The size of HIV epidemics in South Asia depends to a large extent on rates and patterns of partner change—inside and outside commercial sex. Structural factors—including poverty, gender inequality, trafficking, large structured sex work industries, and oscillating migration—influence sexual behaviors and networking patterns.

Similar to the effects of concurrent sexual partnerships, the tendency of IDUs to share needles with others in a network or to use contaminated needles increases the risk of HIV transmission, especially if an injector has an acute HIV infection (MAP 2005). Structural factors, such as drug production and sociopolitical conflict, create the conditions mediating the IDU behavioral factors. Two major drug-producing areas affect South Asia, as depicted in map 2.1 (UNODC 2004), with trafficking routes that transect the entire region. Drug supplies from the Golden Triangle into India's northeastern states and from the Golden Crescent into Afghanistan and Pakistan can account for the IDU-driven HIV epidemics in those regions, thus highlighting a need for multisectoral, regional, and transregional programming.

Map 2.1 Two Major Drug-Producing Areas That Affect South Asia

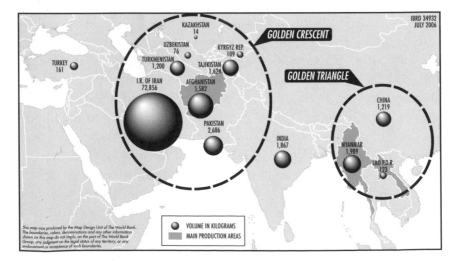

Source: UNODC 2004.

CHAPTER 3

HIV and Related Surveillance in the South Asia Region

By the late 1990s, all five South Asian Region countries included in the core review had established some form of sentinel serological surveillance in adherence with the World Health Organization's recommended practice of collecting and screening anonymous and unlinked blood samples. In addition, Bangladesh, India, and Pakistan have initiated second-generation surveillance and have conducted at least one round of behavioral surveillance. Nepal also intends to launch second-generation surveillance activities but will require more preparation. The content and quality of surveillance vary by country and time.

India

India began surveillance for HIV infection and identification of AIDS cases through 62 public health centers and 9 reference centers in 1987. After the National AIDS Control Organization (NACO) was established five years later, it assumed responsibility for HIV surveillance. NACO gradually expanded the network to comprise 180 sites, the majority of which involved prenatal clinic patients, but by 1999 also involved 77 sites for patients with sexually transmitted infection (STIs) and 9 sites for injecting drug users (IDUs). One year later, NACO added more sites for STI patients, IDUs, and prenatal clinic patients but also started HIV surveillance at one site in Mumbai among female sex workers (SWs) and at three sites in Mumbai, along with sites in Goa and Tamil Nadu, among men having sex with men (MSM). Although the numbers of sites for female SWs and MSM have remained about the same since 2000, those for STI patients, prenatal clinic patients, and (to a lesser extent) IDUs have increased in each annual round (NACO 2005). Table 3.1 summarizes NACO's gradual buildup of its countrywide surveillance system.

As table 3.1 indicates, the scope of surveillance has increased considerably. However, the surveillance coverage in low-prevalence states, especially in northern India, requires urgent improvement, and many more surveillance sites are needed for specific high-risk subgroups, particularly SWs and MSM.

As part of second-generation surveillance and of the national monitoring and evaluation framework, India conducted a baseline behavioral surveillance survey (BSS) among female SWs, their clients, MSM, IDUs, and the general population in 2001 (NACO 2002). As the largest HIV behavioral survey ever undertaken, it comprised 22 sampling units from 34 states and territories and included 84,478 people (almost equally distributed between urban and rural, and between females and males) with 29 and 30 as the mean age for females and males, respectively. NACO also conducted behavioral surveillance among 5,572 female SWs, 5,468 clients of female SWs, 1,355 IDUs, and 1,387 MSM. The monitoring and evaluation framework calls for follow-up BSS in the middle and at the end of the second phase of the National AIDS Control Programme. Although only one national round has been completed, several state-specific BSSs have been conducted.

Table 3.1 HIV Sentinel Surveillance Sites in India

Year	Type of site					Total sites
	Prenatal patient	STI patient	IDU	MSM	Female SW	
1998	94	77	9	0	0	180
1999	94	77	9	0	0	180
2000	118	104	8	2	0	232
2001	173	131	12	2	2	320
2002	173	166	13	3	2	384
2003	271	166	13	3	2	450
2004	272	166	13	3	2	670

Source: NACO 2005.

All of the behavioral and HIV prevalence data in this report are drawn from available national and state BSSs and from other sources where available. For brevity, most subnational data cited generally include only the high- and moderate-prevalence states. NACO (2005) defines the former as a state in which HIV prevalence exceeds 5 percent among high-risk groups and 1 percent among pregnant women. It defines the latter as a state in which HIV prevalence among high-risk groups also exceeds 5 percent but does not exceed 1 percent among pregnant women.

Nepal

Nepal attempted to establish sentinel HIV surveillance in 1991 (NCASC and FHI 2003). The first round was planned to cover female SWs, IDUs, STI patients, and tuberculosis (TB) patients, as well as ANC attenders, from seven sites across the country. However, follow-up surveillance has not occurred systematically. The National Center for AIDS and Sexually Transmitted Disease Control (NCASC) has managed to continue surveillance among STI patients but has not collected data for the past two years. The unavailability of surveillance data has prompted bilateral donors to conduct a series of cross-sectional studies, contributing to the current knowledge of Nepal's HIV situation. After recently reviewing its strategy, NCASC plans to reestablish surveillance with a second-generation system covering STI and TB patients, military service personnel, pregnant women, and blood donors.

Pakistan

Pakistan launched sentinel HIV surveillance in 1986. The current site network consists of the following:

- voluntary counseling and testing centers in all four provinces (Balochistan, Northwest Frontier Province, Punjab, and Sindh)
- all public sector blood banks in all four provinces
- STI clinics in all tertiary-level hospitals in three provinces (Northwest Frontier Province, Punjab, and Sindh).

More recently, the Canadian International Development Agency has supported Pakistan's launch of a second-generation surveillance program that includes these objectives:

- enhanced mapping to determine the locations and sizes of key high-risk networks of female and male SWs, IDUs, and *hijras* (transgendered men)

- integrated biological and behavioral surveillance (IBBS) among high-risk groups to better understand HIV transmission dynamics and epidemic potential.

Pakistan has now completed mapping in several key cities and has initiated IBBS activities; initial successful pilots in Karachi and Rawalpindi were completed in 2004–5. In addition, Pakistan has commissioned additional broader mapping studies, plus biological and behavioral studies with a strong focus on high-risk males.

Bangladesh

Bangladesh began surveillance for HIV infection in 1998 through its National AIDS and Sexually Transmitted Disease Programme (NASP). The surveillance covers FSWs, STI patients, truck drivers, IDUs, MSM, and—to a lesser extent—the general population (NASP 2004). However, all sentinel surveillance sites are in urban areas and locations with HIV prevention programs. Bangladesh has completed five rounds of behavioral surveillance and has made major strides in surveillance, such as pioneering the use of respondent-driven sampling among high-risk groups in South Asia.

Sri Lanka

In 1993, Sri Lanka started sentinel surveillance for HIV infection among FSWs as well as STI and TB patients. Similar to India's evolving sentinel surveillance system, the National Sexually Transmitted Disease and AIDS Control Programme (NSACP) in Sri Lanka gradually expanded its coverage, adding blood donors in 1998, pregnant women in 2000, military service personnel in 2003, and transportation workers and civil service candidates in 2004. Following WHO guidelines to tailor surveillance activities according to the country-specific epidemic, Sri Lanka, with its low-level epidemic, is further expanding its surveillance coverage of high-risk groups and has stopped gathering data on women attending prenatal clinics. To date, most HIV-related behavioral research has been undertaken through cross-sectional studies. However, Sri Lanka is planning to launch baseline BSS among FSWs, military service personnel, police, transportation workers, and internal migrant laborers within two years (NHCPP 2005). Preparation for this task has influenced and enhanced the conduct of sentinel surveillance, shifting sample collection away from clinical facilities and adding new groups to eventually integrate both serological and behavioral surveillance.

Afghanistan, Bhutan, and the Maldives

HIV surveillance is largely limited to incomplete case reporting in each of these three very disparate countries. Afghanistan will undertake behavioral surveillance, perhaps including HIV testing, among IDUs in 2006. In Bhutan, the World Bank–financed HIV/AIDS and STI Prevention and Control Project, which became effective in August 2004, will support improved strategic information systems, including HIV serological and behavioral surveillance and STI surveillance. The 2004 round of sentinel surveillance involved 10 population groups, including the following: prenatal clinic patients, blood donors, STI patients, members of the armed forces, drivers, prisoners, and FSWs.

The royal government of Bhutan has recruited the International Centre for Diarrhoeal Disease Research, Bangladesh (which is implementing serological and behavioral surveillance in Bangladesh), to provide technical assistance in surveillance, monitoring, and evaluation. The government started presurveillance assessment (that is, identification and mapping of high-risk groups) in 2006. It has also revised the design of serological surveys, which had serious limitations in the past because of the small sample sizes of high-risk groups, such as sex workers. The Maldives largely relies on case reporting for surveillance.

CHAPTER 4

Sexual and Injecting Drug Use Behaviors

This chapter analyzes behavioral trends across countries in South Asia. Chapter 6 containing country-specific analysis distills major trends within countries and links them to biological trends and program data.

Female Sex Workers

Behavioral surveillance survey (BSS) data from India (NACO 2001b) and from a cross-sectional study in Sri Lanka (Saravanapavananthan 2002) highlight how client load and consistent condom use may differ according to the type of sex work. India has at least 500,000 female sex workers (SWs), with considerable variation among states. In the 2001 BSS in India, female SWs overall reported a mean of 11 paying clients in the past seven days, a figure that varied among states. Brothel-based female SWs reported a much greater paying client load than their non-brothel-based counterparts.

Likewise in Sri Lanka, which has an estimated 30,000 female SWs and 4,800 brothels countrywide, client load varies by the site of sex work. In Colombo, a higher proportion of brothel-based female SWs than of female SWs based in massage parlors or on the street have two to five clients per day; the female SWs in massage parlors and on the streets report less paying clients.

Within India, the mean number of paying clients in one high-HIV-prevalence state (Maharashtra) and two moderate-prevalence states

(Goa and Gujarat) exceeded the national mean, reflecting in part the importance of brothels as a focus of sex work in these states. In India, a greater proportion of brothel-based female SWs (57 percent) than non-brothel-based female SWs (46 percent) reported using condoms consistently with clients in the past seven days.

Similarly, in Sri Lanka a higher proportion of brothel-based female SWs (38 percent) than massage parlor–based female SWs (10 percent) in Colombo reported consistent condom use. In contrast to the findings of the BSS in India, however, condom use in Sri Lanka did not differ by the type of sex partner. Data from India showed consistent gaps in consistent condom use between paying clients and nonpaying partners, with the widest gap observed in Maharashtra (73 percent condom use for paying clients versus just 7 percent for nonpaying partners) and Tamil Nadu–Pondicherry (54 percent versus 9 percent). Hence, the lower proportion of all female SWs in Colombo that reported consistent condom use may be attributable to infrequent or no condom use with their nonpaying partners. Such behavior suggests that female SWs perceive nonpaying partners as less prone to transmitting HIV. This (mis)perception appears throughout the region, highlighting an important area of focus for prevention programs among female SWs, particularly as those programs mature, to emphasize correct and consistent condom use with both paying clients and nonpaying partners.

Nepal has completed mapping and condom use studies among female SWs. Nepalis refer to female SWs as *bhiringi* (a colloquial term for syphilis) girls (Pike 1999). Many are members of the *Badi* caste from the far western region. *Badi* women historically worked as entertainers, but the scope of their occupation has evolved to include sex work. Mapping studies estimate a high concentration of female SWs (9,600) in the highway districts of Nepal, with a substantial number in the Kathmandu Valley (4,000) and some in Pokhara of the western region (300) (NCASC and FHI 2003). The client load among female SWs from the Kathmandu Valley resembles that among female SWs from Colombo: only 10 percent reported more than five clients per week (Furber, Newell, and Lubben 2002). The proportions of female SWs from the highway districts (52 percent) and Pokhara (72 percent) reporting consistent condom use resemble those across India (FHI 2002).

Like Nepal, Bangladesh has completed mapping and condom use studies among female SWs. Bangladesh has 50,000 to 100,000 female

SWs. Those surveyed reported high client loads and low levels of consistent condom use. Hotel-based female SWs reported the highest client load (44 per week), and their brothel-based and street-based counterparts had lower client loads (18 and 17 clients per week, respectively). Although 85 percent of brothel-based female SWs reported that they had participated in some form of prevention intervention delivered by nongovernmental organizations, consistent condom use was low among new clients (5 percent) and was even lower among regular clients (2.8 percent) (NASP 2004).

Pakistan recently completed a mapping study to estimate the number of female SWs in the country. The study shows dense concentrations of SW networks in some major cities, such as Karachi, Lahore, and Multan (UNICEF and NACP 2002). In those cities, a substantial proportion of female SWs operate from hotels or homes. The home is generally the predominant site for sex work in other cities, except in Hyderabad, which has three times as many street-based as home-based female SWs. Though some cities have established red-light districts, the extralegal status of female SWs, among other things, has driven them to work out of homes or other private facilities. The predominance of home-based sex work in many cities across Pakistan may pose a barrier to traditional prevention interventions designed to reach female SWs who work together in well-defined, readily identifiable public places.

Clients of Female Sex Workers

Estimating the numbers of clients of female SWs is even more problematic than estimating the numbers of female SWs, but in India alone, they clearly are at least in the tens of millions. Cross-sectional studies in South Asian countries of males whose occupations entail travel or extended stays away from their households reveal significant proportions who reported sex with female SWs. Sri Lanka has an estimated 700,000 clients of female SWs, including students, police officers, truck drivers, dockworkers, and sailors (Saravanapavananthan 2002).

In Bangladesh, one study found that 54 percent of truck drivers and rickshaw pullers had sex with at least one female SW in the past year

(Gibney and others 2002). Another study in Nepal showed that the proportions of transportation workers and migrant laborers who had sex with an female SW increased by 20 percentage points for each group within a one-year period (from 42 percent to 62 percent for transportation workers and from 10 percent to 30 percent for migrant laborers between 2000 and 2001) (FHI, New Era, and SACTS 2002a). Both the study in Bangladesh (Gibney and others 2002) and BSS data in India (NACO 2001b) estimated the number of female SWs with whom clients had sex. According to the Bangladesh study, truck drivers and rickshaw pullers reported having sex with a mean of almost two female SWs in the past month and of about five in the past year. In India, clients of female SWs reported having sex with a mean of nearly four female SWs in the past three months, with the highest number reported in Gujarat (6.2). Furthermore, Indian clients reported a greater number of non-brothel-based female SW partners (mean of 4.2) than partners based in brothels (mean of 3.3).

Consistent condom use varies by country, and in India it varies by type of sex partner. In Bangladesh, the NASP cross-sectional study cited earlier, involving transportation industry workers, found low reports of consistent condom use: 2.3 percent of rickshaw pullers and 4.1 percent of truck drivers (NASP 2004). In contrast, in a similar cross-sectional study from Nepal, 60 percent of transportation workers and 45 percent of migrant laborers reported using condoms consistently (FHI, New Era, and SACTS 2002a). Those figures resemble the numbers of clients observed across India, which ranged from as low as 54 percent in Manipur to as high as 77 percent in Maharashtra, with a slight difference between clients who reported sex with brothel-based female SWs (60 percent) and those who reported sex with non-brothel-based female SWs (56 percent). Reports of consistent condom use from clients generally match those reported by female SWs, except in Andhra Pradesh, Karnataka, and Tamil Nadu–Pondicherry, where clients' reports exceed female SW reports by about 10 percent. Behavioral surveillance data from India again highlights a variation in consistent condom use by the type of sex partner. Analogous to female SWs using condoms less frequently among noncommercial partners, consistent use of condoms by clients of female SWs is less likely with more regular female partners who are not engaged in sex work, perhaps because clients perceive sex with them as less risky.

Men Having Sex with Men

Mapping studies from Pakistan demonstrate that, as with female SWs, large urban areas contain dense concentrations of men having sex with men (MSM) and male SWs (MSW). Those studies suggest that Karachi has almost 5,000 male SWs and 7,626 *hijras* (NACP 2005a), whereas Lahore has 7,500 male SWs and 2,000 *hijras* (NACP and Naz Foundation International 2005). These sites are therefore appropriate for HIV and second-generation surveillance among MSM, which Pakistan has initiated through the selection of populous cities for both serological and behavioral surveillance.

BSS data from India (NACO 2001c) highlight that among partners of MSM, a greater proportion are male SWs. Contrary to the trend observed among female SWs and their clients, a higher proportion of MSM reported consistent condom use with partners who are not engaged in sex work than with male SW partners in every site except Delhi, where the difference was minimal.

Findings from a cross-sectional study among MSM in Sri Lanka (Saravanapavananthan 2002) indicated that partner load varies by site. Generally, MSM identified at clinics for sexually transmitted infection (STI) patients were more likely than their counterparts in gay support groups and other locations to report fewer lifetime sex partners (45 percent of MSM STI patients reported fewer than two lifetime sex partners versus 69 percent of MSM from other locations, who had more than 10 such partners) and fewer same-sex partners in the past 12 months (65 percent of MSM STI patients reported fewer than two male sex partners, versus 44 percent of MSM from other locations, who reported sex with more than 10 males). The study also noted that in each site-specific MSM group, some identified themselves as bisexual.

Bisexual behavior is observed in two groups of studies. First, cross-sectional studies from Bangladesh (Gibney and others 2002) and Pakistan (Baqi and others 1999; Khan 1996; Mirza and Hasnain 1995), as well as BSS data from India (NACO 2001c), reveal that clients of female SWs also have sex with men. In Bangladesh, 7 percent of rickshaw pullers and truck drivers reported sex with a male SW in the past year, and 21 percent of them reported sex with a male SW at least once in their lifetime. Similarly, in Pakistan, 39 percent of clients of female SWs are also clients of male SWs, and 30 percent of male STI patients have sex with males. Across India, 29 percent of clients of female SWs reported sex with at least one male partner in the past 12 months; a greater proportion of those who were clients of brothel-based female SWs (37 percent) versus clients of non-brothel-based female SWs (26 percent) reported such behavior. By state, percentages ranged from 16 percent in Manipur to over 45 percent in Maharashtra, Goa, and Gujarat. Reports of consistent condom use also varied. In Maharashtra, Tamil Nadu–Pondicherry, and Gujarat, about a third of clients of female SWs reported consistent condom use with their male partners.

Second, to exemplify another manifestation of bisexual behavior, BSS data from India also indicated that about a quarter or more of MSM in all sites except for Karnataka reported having sex with at least one female in the past six months, with a mean of about one to three partners. Just as MSM are less likely to use condoms consistently with male partners who are not engaged in sex work than with male sex workers, they also reported lower consistent condom use with female partners, not exceeding 26 percent in any site. The low reports of consistent condom use by MSM with female partners may suggest that for MSM in India, female partners are perceived as less risky for HIV transmission but these female partners represent a potential bridge for HIV and STI transmission to the general population.

General Population

Aside from those studies in India, behavioral surveillance of general population groups in other South Asian countries is limited. As part of the BSS in India, men and women in the general population in urban and rural areas were asked about the extent to which they had sex with nonregular partners and used condoms consistently with those partners (NACO 2001a). The data revealed considerable variability among states and between rural and urban areas. Across the country, 7 percent of men and women reported having sex with nonregular partners in the past 12 months, 12 percent among men and 2 percent among women. Commercial sex was not explicitly asked about, but this disparity between men and women suggests that the majority of nonregular partners of men are sex workers. In two of the five high-HIV-prevalence states, Andhra Pradesh and Maharashtra, and two moderate-prevalence states, Goa and Gujarat, sex with nonregular partners was reported more frequently than the national mean. In Maharashtra, a greater proportion of urban males than their rural counterparts reported having sex with nonregular partners (23 percent versus 10 percent), but the opposite urban-rural divide was reported in other states, although the differences are small. High levels of risky sex reported from rural areas, exemplified by rural males reporting nonregular sexual partnerships (for example, 21.7 percent in Andhra Pradesh, 14.0 percent in Goa-Daman-Diu, and 17.2 percent in Gujarat-Dadra-Nagar Haveli), contribute to the epidemic potential of HIV in India.

Throughout India, less than a third of the general population who reported sex with nonregular partners also reported using condoms consistently with those partners, with notable exceptions in Maharashtra and Goa-Daman-Diu. Both urban and rural dwellers in those two areas reported comparatively high levels of consistent condom use with nonregular partners. In urban areas, well over half of the general population reported such condom use, with proportionately greater reports (generally by at least 20 percent) of males reporting condom use than females. In Goa-Daman-Diu, a relatively high proportion of rural males (70 percent) reported consistent condom use with nonregular partners, whereas no females reported such condom use. The opposite trend occurred in Maharashtra, where a slightly greater proportion of rural females (42 percent) than rural males (38 percent) reported using condoms with nonregular partners.

Injecting Drug Users

Drug use patterns vary greatly across the South Asia Region. Sri Lanka is estimated to have 40,000 to 50,000 drug users (Pattern of Drug Abuse 2003). One cross-sectional study highlights that among individuals arrested for drug-related offenses, about 75 percent of males and 100 percent of females preferred heroin, and nearly 60 percent of males and over 95 percent of females had used drugs for at least six years (Pattern of Drug Abuse 2003). Among those imprisoned for such charges, only 2 percent of heroin users injected the drug.

Conversely, most Bangladeshi injecting drug users (IDUs) began using drugs through other means and eventually adopted injecting as their primary mode of drug use (NASP 2004). Heroin was introduced to Nepal in the 1960s, but buprenorphine (brand name Tidigesic) replaced it as the drug of choice in the 1990s because of its lower price (one-eighth of the cost of heroin) and comparable ability to induce a high after injecting (Reid and Costigan 2002). In Nepal, the epidemic among IDUs is concentrated in Kathmandu, Pokhara in the Western region, and in the three terai districts in the Eastern region. The Centre for Research on Environment, Health and Population Activities (CREHPA), in partnership with the National Centre for AIDS and STD Control (NCASC) and Family Health International (FHI), has conducted several ethnographic studies of injecting and sexual behaviors of IDUs throughout the country, reporting estimates of 4,399 IDUs in Kathmandu Valley and 585 IDUs in Pokhara (FHI and CREHPA 2004). These studies also reported estimates of 600 IDUs in Biratnagar, 901 IDUs in Dharan, and 525 IDUs in Jhapa, all of which are in Nepal's Eastern region. Drug supplies for the latter two western and eastern regions are imported from bordering towns in India. Drugs supplied from India's border areas with Bangladesh could also have played a role in the emergence of IDUs in that country, estimated at 20,000 in Dhaka, Rajshahi, and other towns in the border areas (personal communication, Department of Narcotics Control).

Straddled between Afghanistan and India, Pakistan has about 500,000 chronic heroin users, of whom 15 percent report injecting as their primary mode of use (UNODC 2002). Mapping studies show that IDUs, like female SWs and MSM, are highly concentrated in Karachi, which has as many as 3,200 home-based IDUs and almost four times as many street-based IDUs (NACP 2005a).

Cross-sectional studies from Pakistan (Altaf, Shah, and Memon 2003; Ghauri, Shah, and Memon 2003; Zafar and others 2003) and behavioral surveillance from India (NACO 2001c) show that most IDUs exchange drugs and equipment, increasing their HIV risk. A substantial proportion of IDUs in Pakistan (40 to 77 percent) and in India (50 to 70 percent, except in West Bengal) used a needle and syringe previously used by someone else. From 60 to 80 percent injected drugs in a group setting, where drugs and contaminated equipment are more likely shared. Well over half of IDUs, except in West Bengal, loaned, rented, or sold a used needle and syringe in the past month. A consistently greater proportion of IDUs in Manipur and Tamil Nadu also reported using prefilled syringes (almost 30 percent in both cities versus

20 percent overall); using syringes squirted from another (slightly over 40 percent in Manipur and 50 percent in Tamil Nadu versus 31 percent overall); and sharing cookers, vials, containers, filters, or rinse water (about 65 percent in both cities versus 47 percent overall) in the past month. A high proportion of IDUs in Manipur (68 percent) and Tamil Nadu (62 percent), but especially in Maharashtra (82 percent), reported drawing drug solution from a common container in the past month. Both Bangladesh and Pakistan feature "street doctors," or professional injectors, who receive payment from IDUs for injections but typically use the same needle and syringe for multiple IDUs. In Pakistan, a substantial proportion of IDUs (from as low as 37 percent to as high as 80 percent) received injections from street doctors.

Preliminary data in Afghanistan show that, of an estimated 920,000 illicit drug users (3.8 percent of the total population), 120,000 are women (2.1 percent of the total adult female population) and 60,000 are children (0.7 percent of all children) (UNODC 2005b). An estimated 50,000 are heroin users; of those, 15 percent of males inject. No females reported injecting drugs, but data from drug treatment centers indicate that a low rate (less than 1 percent of female users) inject. The rate of needle sharing varied, with about 90 percent (8 out of 9) of opium users, 70 percent (28 of 39) of heroin users, and 25 percent (11 of 46) of pharmaceutical users sharing needles with others. The drug use problem is highest in the north and central parts of the country. Although injecting drug use is mainly an urban problem, drug use is widespread in both urban and rural areas. Between 1989 and 2005 the Central Blood Bank, Kabul, reported 67 HIV-positive cases out of 125,832 blood samples screened at central and provincial levels (Islamic Republic of Afghanistan 2006). In one community profile of drug users in Afghanistan, almost half of all heroin users started their practices while in Iran or Pakistan (GTZ 2005). Few harm reduction programs, including needle exchange, are in place to break transmission of HIV/AIDS.

Female Sex Workers, Clients, and MSM Who Also Inject Drugs

Although FSWs and MSM are already considered at high risk for HIV transmission, they can increase their risk for HIV transmission by injecting drugs. One cross-sectional study examined sex work and drug use in Pakistan (NACP 2005b). According to the study, 3 percent of the female SWs in the sample were also IDUs, probably through exposure to drug use through their sex partners: 21 percent of the female SWs reported sex with IDU clients, and 15 percent of them reported sex with nonpaying IDU partners. From the BSS in India, about 6 percent of female SWs overall reported having ever tried any "illicit" drug, and about one-third of those (2 percent overall) reported injecting drugs in the past year. Throughout India, about 2 percent of clients of female SWs also reported injecting drugs in the past year. The corresponding figures for both female SWs and their clients were much higher in the northeast. For example, in Manipur, 19 percent of female SWs and 11 percent of clients reported injecting drugs in the past year. For female SWs and their clients, injecting drug use appears to occur more frequently outside of brothel settings. By state, Manipur has the highest proportion of female SWs and clients who reported injecting drugs. Among MSM, those in Karnataka and Tamil Nadu–Pondicherry accounted for most of the injecting drug use behavior observed overall (NACO 2001b for FSWs and their clients; NACO 2001c for MSM).

IDUs Who Also Have Risky Sex

Although IDUs constitute a high-risk group because of their drug- and equipment-sharing behaviors, they can also increase their HIV risk by practicing unsafe sex. One cross-sectional study in Pokhara, Nepal, found that one in three IDUs had sex with at least one female SW in the past 12 months, and 70 percent of those had sex with more than two female SWs (FHI and NCASC 2002; FHI, New Era, and SACTS 2003b). According to cross-sectional studies from Pakistan (Altaf, Shah, and Memon 2003; Ghauri, Shah, and Memon 2003; Zafar and others 2003), at least one-fifth of IDUs reported having sex with female SWs, and well over half had never used condoms with any previous sex partner. The BSS in India collected similar data by different types of partners (NACO 2001c). Greater proportions of IDUs in every state reported having sex with regular partners than with female SWs or nonregular partners. Possibly because IDUs also attribute a lower risk to greater regularity of their sex partners, they were less likely to report using condoms consistently with regular partners than with female SWs or nonregular partners.

CHAPTER 5

HIV Prevalence and Spread

Female Sex Workers

Data on HIV prevalence among female sex workers (SWs) underscore the remarkable heterogeneity of HIV in the South Asia Region. In India, HIV prevalence among female SWs sampled in Bangalore, Karnataka, was 14 percent in 2003 and 22 percent in 2004, but it is unclear whether those samples are comparable (KSAPS and ICHAP 2003, 2004). A recent survey of female SWs in Mysore, also in Karnataka, found an HIV prevalence of about 25 percent (Reza Paul and others 2005). In Mumbai, HIV prevalence among female SWs has ranged from 45 to 60 percent between 2000 and 2004 (NACO 2005).

Some areas of Nepal have an advanced HIV epidemic among female SWs. The 2001 HIV prevalence among female SWs in the Kathmandu Valley (16 percent) is slightly higher than the figure among Karnataka's female SWs in 2004 (NCASC and FHI 2002b). However, it is nearly three times higher for Nepali female SWs who have worked in parts of India other than Mumbai (41 percent) and almost five times higher for those who have worked in Mumbai (72 percent) (FHI, New Era, and SACTS 2002b). Every year, between 5,000 and 7,000 Nepali girls are trafficked to India, where at least 20,000 female SWs come from Nepal (Furber, Newell, and Lubben 2002). Given the high HIV prevalence among female SWs in India, especially Mumbai, plus the additional marginalization that Nepali girls and women face, these data suggest that sex work in India greatly increases their risk for HIV infection.

Recent HIV prevalence figures among segments of female SW sub-populations in Pakistan and Bangladesh are lower than among comparable groups in India. In Pakistan, HIV prevalence among female SWs was 0.5 percent in Lahore and 0 percent in Karachi (NACP 2005b). With an emerging epidemic, Bangladesh disaggregated its surveillance of female SWs by the type of site of sex work. In the sixth surveillance round in 2005, HIV prevalence was 0.2 percent among brothel-based female SWs, 0 to 0.2 percent among street-based sex workers, 0 to 0.6 percent among hotel-based sex workers, and 0 to 1.7 percent among casual sex workers limited to the North-West-K district (NASP 2005).

Classified as having a low-level epidemic, Sri Lanka underwent annual rounds of sentinel surveillance in each province between 2000 and 2004. Those surveys found that HIV prevalence among female SWs has generally not exceeded 1 percent (NSACP 2005). Similarly, HIV infection rates among female SWs in Pakistan remain low, but a significant nexus between female SWs and injecting drug users (IDUs) suggests that infections from injecting drug use may lead to increased numbers of sexually transmitted HIV infections as well.

Men Having Sex with Men

Data on HIV prevalence among men having sex with men (MSM) in the South Asia Region are scarce, and more efforts to collect such data have been undertaken. Biobehavioral surveillance in Pakistan revealed that HIV prevalence was 2 percent among *hijras* and 4 percent among male SWs in Karachi. It was 0 percent among *hijras* and 0.5 percent among male SWs in Lahore (NACP 2005b). Sentinel surveillance data from Bangladesh indicate that, similar to infection rates among female SWs, the HIV epidemic remains at a low level among MSM, with a prevalence of 0 percent among MSM, 0.3 percent among male SWs, and 0.8 percent among *hijras* (NASP 2005). In contrast, HIV prevalence rates among MSM in Goa, Mumbai, and Tamil Nadu have ranged from 2 percent to over 50 percent in samples at different times. Those extreme fluctuations may be due to a combination of small sample sizes and different sampling methodologies from year to year. Much more data are needed to understand the extent to which the HIV epidemic has reached the MSM community in general in Goa, Mumbai, and Tamil Nadu.

Injecting Drug Users

The efficiency of HIV transmission through injecting drug use behaviors and networks can accelerate the growth of HIV epidemics among IDUs. For example, during 2004, serological surveillance data collected by provincial AIDS control programs in Pakistan found an increase in HIV prevalence among IDUs from 0.4 percent at the beginning of the year to 10 percent by December (NACP 2004), indicating how rapidly and explosively HIV can spread through injecting drug use. One study in Nepal also documented rapid rises in HIV prevalence among IDUs between 1991 and 2002: from 2 percent to 68 percent in the Kathmandu Valley and from 0 percent to 22 percent in Pokhara in the western region (NCASC and FHI 2003). Jhapa, a town in the eastern region with a significant IDU community, had an HIV prevalence of 35 percent among IDUs in 2003 (FHI, New Era, and SACTS 2003a).

Sentinel surveillance from Bangladesh showed that HIV prevalence grew for several years among IDUs in the central region while remaining low in the northwest and southeast, illustrating both the potential and heterogeneity of transmission in the country (NASP 2005). However, according to the recent sixth round of surveillance, HIV prevalence has started to rise in both the southeast and northwest, indicating that low HIV prevalence among IDUs offers at best a brief window for prevention programming. Figure 5.1 summarizes the HIV prevalence trends among IDUs in Bangladesh. HIV infection occurs largely among male IDUs at present, though it has begun to appear among male heroin smokers, as shown in figure 5.2 for one central district neighborhood in Bangladesh.

As shown in table 5.1, HIV infection was highly concentrated in two neighborhoods in Bangladesh, underscoring the local heterogeneity of HIV transmission, the potential for rapid diffusion upon the introduction of HIV into drug-using neighborhoods, and the opportunity for focused prevention and treatment programs (NASP 2005).

Figure 5.1 HIV Prevalence among IDUs in Bangladesh

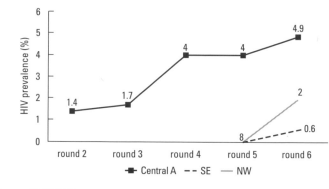

Source: NASP 2005.

Figure 5.2 HIV Infection among Male and Female IDUs and Male Heroin Smokers in Central District in Bangladesh

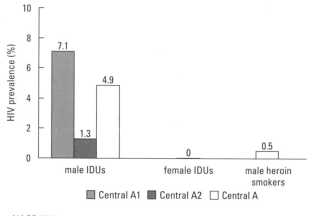

Source: NASP 2005.
Note: IDU = injecting drug users

Female IDUs in Bangladesh currently have low HIV prevalence levels, which could explain why HIV transmission through sex work remains limited. However, a major nexus between injecting drug use and sex work exists: over 60 percent of female IDUs are also female SWs. These women reported an average of 10 clients in the past week, and almost 45 percent reported that they relied on sex work as their principal source of income in the past six months (NASP 2005). In addition, nearly half of female IDUs are also married or currently live with their regular sex partners, who constitute a bridge population.

Table 5.1 Variations in HIV Infection in Seven Neighborhoods in Bangladesh

Neighborhood	Sample size	HIV infection rate	
		Number of cases	Percentage of sample
1	157	14	8.9
2	94	2	2.1
3	59	0	0.0
4	25	0	0.0
5	24	0	0.0
6	32	0	0.0
7	13	0	0.0
Total	404	16	4.0

Source: NASP 2005.

By 2000, India's sentinel surveillance program had established that its northeastern region is experiencing IDU-driven HIV epidemics, with HIV prevalence of over 50 percent among IDUs in Manipur and similarly high figures for Nagaland and Mizoram. Prevalence in Manipur has declined since then but still remains over 20 percent. As described previously, a substantial proportion of IDUs in Manipur inject with used needles and syringes and prefilled or squirted syringes, share equipment, and engage in other risky network drug use practices. Such practices fuel the HIV epidemic's growth. In some northeastern districts bordering Myanmar, which has Asia's most severe HIV epidemic among IDUs, HIV prevalence as high as 8 percent has been reported among prenatal clinic patients. These rates illustrate how injecting drug use can ignite a wider HIV epidemic, quite literally injecting HIV into sexual networks. HIV prevalence is also high among IDUs in Delhi, Mumbai, and Tamil Nadu (NACO 2005).

Other High-Risk Male Groups

As shown in the figure 5.3, HIV infection among truckers in several sites in India rose steeply from 1994 to 1997, suggesting that truckers are more likely to engage in unsafe sex than men in the general population and demonstrating the potential for a significant increase in infection among men at elevated risk. Though truckers remain at higher risk, large-scale targeted interventions promoting safer sexual practices may subsequently have reduced their risk, particularly in

Figure 5.3   HIV among Truckers in Selected Indian Sites, 1994–97

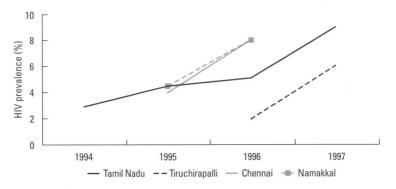

Source: NACO 2005.

Tamil Nadu, where a recent survey found a decline in the reported number of nonregular sex partners (from 48 percent in 1996 to 34 percent in 2004). That survey also found that 90 percent of truckers' contacts with commercial sex partners were associated with condom use (APAC 2004).

In Bangladesh, HIV prevalence remains low among high-risk male groups, such as 0.5 percent among male heroin smokers and 0 to 0.8 percent among MSM, as noted previously. Among large samples of male truckers, rickshaw pullers, and dockworkers, HIV prevalence has remained relatively stable, ranging from 0.4 to 0.6 percent (NASP 2005).

General Population

Most estimates of HIV prevalence in the general population derive from sentinel surveillance among women attending prenatal clinics, a source that can bias estimates in both directions. On the one hand, data from such clinics could underestimate HIV prevalence in the general population because they exclude men and female SWs (especially older women who tend not to visit prenatal facilities), both of which may have higher HIV prevalence. On the other hand, data from prenatal clinics could overestimate HIV prevalence in the general population because they reflect an oversampling of urban areas. Similarly, in India, a significant proportion of women (mean age of 25) undergo tubal ligation; hence, women presenting at prenatal clinics may represent a younger age distribution, which could result in bias toward higher HIV prevalence than in the general population. Global experience, based largely on data from Africa, suggests that data from prenatal clinics tend to overestimate HIV prevalence in general populations. Whether this pattern also applies to South Asia is uncertain.

Data from Tamil Nadu in India allow a comparison of prenatal clinic and population-based data. Figure 5.5 compares several years of prenatal data in Tamil Nadu and one round of population-based data, suggesting that, overall, HIV prevalence findings from both sources are similar. However, a gender-disaggregated analysis of population-based data, as shown in figure 5.6, shows higher HIV prevalence among men and suggests that data from prenatal clinics may underestimate HIV prevalence in the general population.

Data from Bagalkot, a district in northern Karnataka, India, with high HIV prevalence, suggest that estimates of HIV prevalence from prenatal clinic and population-based sources may be broadly comparable (figure 5.6).

India's National AIDS Control Organization (NACO) has collected a wealth of HIV prevalence data from prenatal clinic clients over several years through its sentinel surveillance system. In four high-prevalence states (Andhra Pradesh, Karnataka, Maharashtra, and Tamil Nadu), IIIV prevalence among such clients has generally

Figure 5.4 Prenatal Clinic and Population-Based HIV Prevalence in Tamil Nadu, India

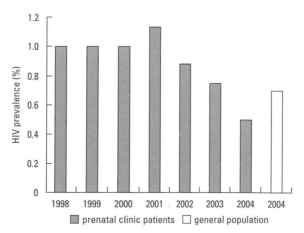

Source: APAC 2005a, b; NACO 2005.

Figure 5.5 Population-Based HIV Prevalence among Men and Women in Tamil Nadu, India

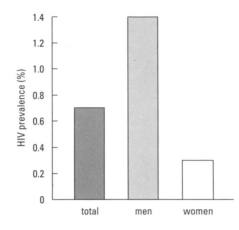

Source: APAC 2005b.

Figure 5.6 HIV Prevalence in Bagalkot, Karnataka, India

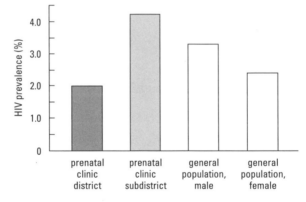

Source: Blanchard and others 2005.

ranged from 1 to 2 percent since 2000, with the prevalence in Tamil Nadu seeming to decline in recent years (NACO 2005). Recent data suggest that HIV prevalence among prenatal clinic patients may be decreasing—or at least stabilizing—in southern states, whereas it may be increasing slightly in northern states, although the epidemic there remains at a relatively low level. In the northeastern states of Manipur and Nagaland, with IDU-driven HIV epidemics, HIV prevalence among prenatal clinic patients has ranged from 1 percent to 1.5 percent, but temporal trends are difficult to ascertain because of changes in surveillance sites and sampling methodologies over time.

Compared with the scale and consistency of prenatal clinic data collection, few population-based surveys have been conducted to estimate HIV prevalence among the general population, but findings from the surveys that exist have highlighted remarkable local heterogeneity. HIV prevalence can vary between districts within states and even between *talukas* and villages within districts. For example, in the southern Indian state of Karnataka, HIV prevalence ranges from less than 1 percent in roughly half of the districts to over 3 percent for some northern districts (KSAPS and ICHAP 2004). In one such northern district, Bagalkot, a population-based survey conducted in 2003 showed differences by residence, *taluka*, and village (ICHAP 2004). Rural residents had a higher HIV prevalence than their urban counterparts (3.6 versus 2.4 percent). HIV prevalence ranged from 1.2 to 4.9 percent in the three sampled *talukas* and from 0 to 8.2 percent in the 10 sampled villages.

No data regarding HIV prevalence in the general population are available from Nepal, which vitiates a confident interpretation of the country's HIV epidemic. In Pakistan, HIV prevalence in the general population remains close to zero (as approximated using professional blood donors, though notwithstanding the potential upward bias of estimates based on this group). In Bangladesh, recent studies among samples of rural men and women living in the Matlab region and among a "general" population of women attending a health care clinic in Dhaka have not found any HIV cases (NASP 2005). Estimates from Sri Lanka reinforce its categorization as a country with a low-level epidemic; in 2004, HIV prevalence among prenatal clinic patients was 0.14 percent, despite significant levels of herpes simplex virus–type 2 (NSACP 2005). Bhutan's 2004 round of sentinel surveillance showed similarly low HIV prevalence among prenatal clinic patients and blood donors: 0.04 and 0 percent, respectively (U.S. Bureau of the Census 2006). Neither Afghanistan nor the Maldives has undertaken efforts to estimate HIV prevalence in the general population.

CHAPTER 6

Country-Specific Analyses

The country analyses have been undertaken following reviews of available published and unpublished literature. In addition, members of the team of authors made country visits to Afghanistan, Bangladesh, India, Nepal, Pakistan, and Sri Lanka, to interview key informants from governmental agencies, nongovernmental organizations, and international agencies. Unpublished reports were also gathered during these country visits. Data analysis and interpretation are the responsibility of the authors.

India

Epidemic Overview

With approximately 40 percent of all of Asia's population, India has more than 60 percent of the continent's estimated HIV infections (UNAIDS 2004). The scale and heterogeneity of the country's HIV epidemic can be appreciated by considering how India's size and complexity resemble those of a continent in which some states and even districts are larger than many African countries.

India's epidemic is concentrated in eight states with over 1 percent HIV prevalence in prenatal clinics (NACO 2005):

- Tamil Nadu, Karnataka, and Andhra Pradesh in the south

- Maharashtra and Goa in the west

- Manipur, Nagaland, and Mizoram in the northeast.

The eight states contain less than 30 percent of India's population but almost 70 percent of its HIV cases. Figures 6.1 and 6.2 show that overall HIV prevalence in those states is at least fivefold higher than in the rest of India (Kumar and others 2005, 58–73).

Differences in HIV prevalence mirror variations in sexual risk behaviors. For example, as shown in figures 6.3 and 6.4, men and

Figure 6.1 Comparison of State-Specific and National HIV Prevalence

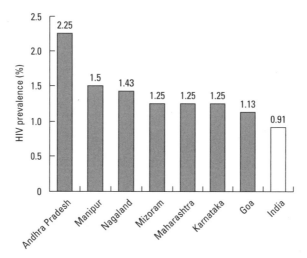

Source: NACO 2005.

Figure 6.2 HIV Prevalence in State Clusters in India, 1998–2003

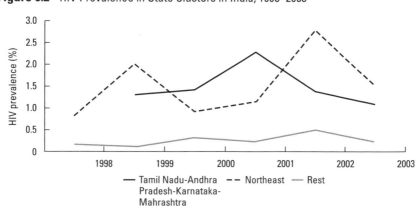

Source: Kumar and others 2005, page 61.

Figure 6.3 Sexual Partners in Previous Year among Men Reporting at least One Sex Partner in State Clusters in India

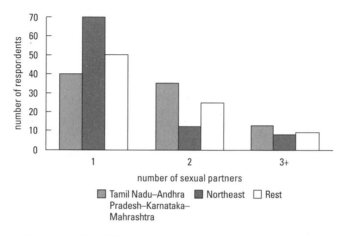

number of sexual partners

■ Tamil Nadu–Andhra Pradesh–Karnataka–Mahrashtra   ■ Northeast   □ Rest

Source: Kumar and others 2005, page 64.

Figure 6.4 Sexual Partners in Previous Year among Women Reporting at least One Sex Partner in State Clusters in India

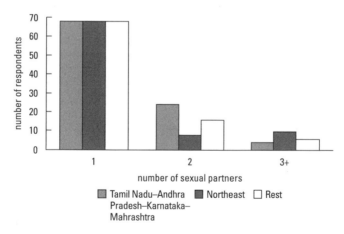

number of sexual partners

■ Tamil Nadu–Andhra Pradesh–Karnataka–Mahrashtra   ■ Northeast   □ Rest

Source: Kumar and others 2005, page 64.

women in the south and west, as well as northeast clusters, tend to report higher numbers of sexual partners in the previous year (Kumar and others 2005, 58–73).

Further analysis of India's epidemic suggests a concentration of HIV infection in a set of districts in the eight states. District mapping indicates three major foci for HIV transmission in India, specifically the following:

- northern Karnataka–southern Maharashtra corridor

- coastal Andhra Pradesh

- northeastern states bordering Myanmar with high injecting drug use.

Figures 6.5, 6.6, and 6.7 present district-level data from prenatal clinic patients and one set of blood donors in the northeast (NACO 2005).

A Case Study in Heterogeneity: Bagalkot District, India

As emphasized earlier, large observed differences in HIV prevalence among states and among districts within states characterize the HIV epidemic in India, and a consideration of how this heterogeneity has emerged is important. Possibly the variation could simply reflect different times of introduction of HIV, but the high level of mobility in India makes that explanation increasingly implausible. A more likely explanation relates to how differences in the underlying sexual structure (that is, sexual behaviors and networks) among locations drive the observed epidemiological heterogeneity. To better understand possible sources of heterogeneity in HIV transmission dynamics, we have undertaken a detailed analysis of sexual structure and HIV epidemiology in Bagalkot, one high-prevalence district in southern India.

Bagalkot, a district in northern Karnataka, has a population of 1.65 million, 71 percent of whom live in rural areas. Its main industry is

Figure 6.5 HIV Prevalence among Pregnant Women in Districts of Karnataka-Maharashtra Corridor, India, 2003–2004

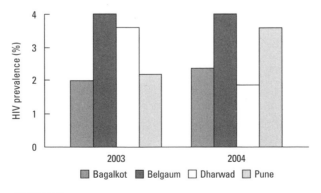

Source: NACO 2005.

Figure 6.6 HIV Prevalence among Pregnant Women in Coastal Andhra
Pradesh, India, 2003–2004

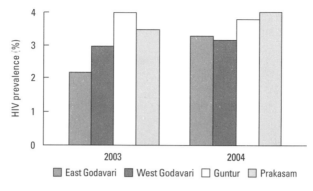

Source: NACO 2005.

Figure 6.7 HIV Prevalence among Pregnant Women and Voluntary Blood Donors in
Northeastern States, India

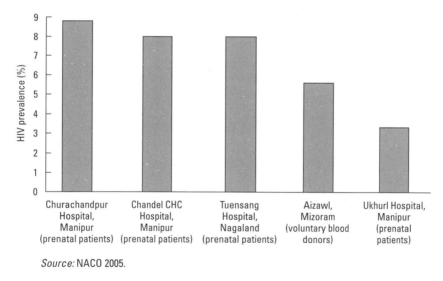

Source: NACO 2005.

agriculture, and 65 percent of the working population engages in agri-
cultural cultivation. Because some parts are irrigated and others are
more drought prone, economic production varies within the district.
Many of the nonagricultural workers are employed as laborers in min-
ing, another main industry for the district. Bagalkot is divided into six
talukas, which are subdistrict administrative blocks. This case study

focuses on three adjacent *talukas*, as shown in map 6.1. These *talukas* have a combined population of 810,100, which is distributed across 241 villages and 6 urban centers.

Three sources of data are analyzed and used:

• a detailed mapping and enumeration of female sex workers (SWs) in all 247 villages and urban areas

• a set of "polling booth" surveys of sexual behaviors in a random sample of village-dwelling men

• a population-based sample survey of HIV prevalence.

HIV Epidemiology   Routine sentinel surveillance data from 2002 to 2004 ($n = 2,400$) indicate that the overall HIV prevalence among prenatal clinic patients was 3.1 percent (KSAPS and ICHAP 2002, 2003, 2004). The prevalence did not differ significantly between those in rural (3.4 percent) and those in urban areas (3.0 percent). A population-based HIV prevalence study was conducted in 2003 in the three focus *talukas*. The study, which was based on a random cluster sampling of 10 villages and 20 urban blocks ($n = 4,007$), showed an overall HIV prevalence of 2.9 percent, higher among males than females ($p = 0.10$) and significantly higher in rural than in urban areas ($p < 0.05$), as shown in figure 6.8 (ICHAP 2004).

Map 6.1   Bagalkot District, Karnataka, India

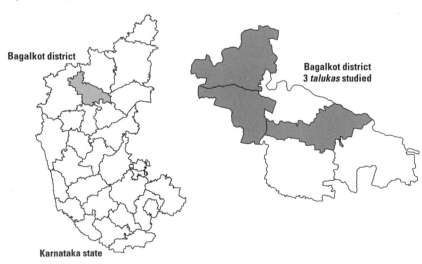

Figure 6.8 HIV Prevalence in Three *Talukas* in Bagalkot from a Population-Based Survey

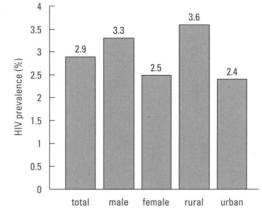

Source: ICHAP 2004.

Interestingly, the overall HIV prevalence among female survey participants was somewhat lower than the sentinel prenatal clinic samples. HIV prevalence differed significantly among the three *talukas*, ranging from 1.2 percent in *taluka* A to 4.9 percent in *taluka* C. Those differences are even more pronounced in rural areas, with HIV prevalence ranging from 1.4 percent in *taluka* A to 6.0 percent in *taluka* C. The substantial variations in HIV prevalence in areas of such close geographic proximity suggest differences in the epidemic potential, rather than the epidemic phase.

Sexual Structure To better understand the reasons for such substantial variations in HIV prevalence among the three *talukas*, the sexual structure was examined more closely, with a particular emphasis on the volume and distribution of female sex work and male sexual behaviors. A detailed mapping and enumeration of female SWs in all villages and urban areas showed substantial differences in the volume and distribution of these women. Overall, *taluka* A had an estimated 295 female SWs, or approximately 4.2 per 1,000 adults. In contrast, *talukas* B (1,927 female SWs; 10.4 per 1,000 adults) and C (1,269 female SWs; 12.6 per 1,000 adults) had substantially more female SWs in both absolute and relative terms. Moreover, as shown in figure 6.9, female SWs were much more widely distributed in the villages of *talukas* B and C compared with *taluka* A. Only 15 percent of villages in *taluka* A

Figure 6.9 Distribution of Female Sex Workers in Villages of Three *Talukas*, Bagalkot, Karnataka, India, 2004

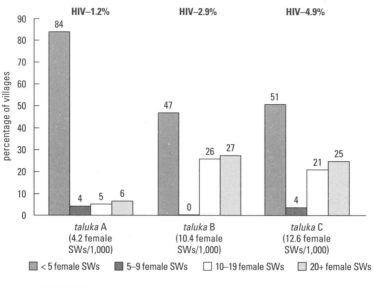

Source: ICHAP 2004.

had at least five female SWs, compared with 43 percent of villages in B and 49 percent in C. Only 6 percent of villages in *taluka* A had 20 or more female SWs, compared with 27 percent and 25 percent in *talukas* B and C, respectively.

Female SWs in *talukas* B and C also had a higher client volume than those in *taluka* A, as shown in figure 6.10.

Self-reported male sexual behavior also differed substantially between the three *talukas*. Specifically, a higher proportion of men in *talukas* B and C reported ever having a nonmarital commercial or noncommercial sexual partner, as shown in figure 6.11.

These sets of data from Bagalkot district provide several important insights.

• First, HIV prevalence is as high or higher in rural areas as in urban areas, suggesting that the sexual structure in rural areas in terms of sexual behaviors and networks is sufficient to sustain and amplify HIV transmission.

Figure 6.10 Weekly Client Volume among FSWs in Three *Talukas*, Bagalkot, Karnataka, India, 2004

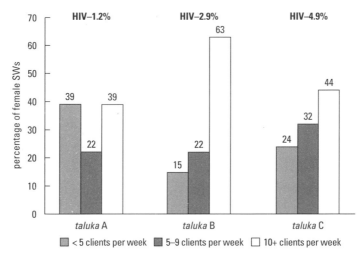

Source: ICHAP 2004.

Figure 6.11 Proportion of Men Who Reported Ever Having a Nonmarital Sexual Partner, Bagalkot, Karnataka, India, 2004

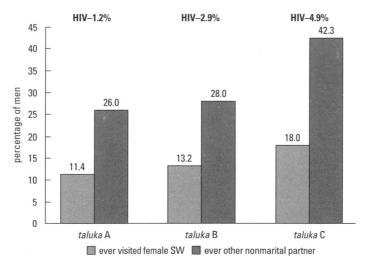

Source: ICHAP 2004.

- Second, even within this small geographic area, substantial hetero-geneity exists in the HIV epidemic, suggesting that heterogeneity in transmission dynamics occurs at a very local level.

- Third, local areas exhibit highly variable sexual structures, most likely associated with differences in the nature of locally concen-trated epidemics. In particular, large differences in the volume and distribution of female sex work could relate to variations in the pat-terns of sexual behavior among men.

Together, those findings suggest that differences in sexual struc-tures and transmission dynamics, rather than epidemic phase, can explain the observed heterogeneity in the prevalence of HIV within India. Consequently, the epidemic potential will differ, underscoring the strategic importance of identifying and focusing prevention pro-grams on those local areas where the epidemic is likely to be the most severe. That strategy will require the development of rapid assessment tools that can pinpoint such pockets of higher risk and the application of those tools widely in both urban and rural areas, to ensure adequate coverage of focused prevention programs. In addition, further detailed research in local areas in Karnataka and in other Indian states is required to verify these findings and to increase our understanding of both HIV transmission dynamics and appropriate responses.

Analysis of the HIV Epidemic in India

The preceding analysis supports the view that India's highly heteroge-neous epidemic poses its greatest risk and challenge in the form of a large number of *local concentrated* epidemics. Mapping studies provide some evidence of substantial pockets of high-risk networks in many locations in India. Most of those networks involve female sex work, but growing evidence also suggests that high-risk networks of men having sex with men (MSM) may play an important role for HIV transmission dynamics in many locations. Injecting drug user (IDU) networks are still primarily concentrated in the northeastern states (Manipur, Mizo-ram, and Nagaland), where they have ignited major epidemics, but substantial pockets of those networks also appear in some major cities of the southern and western states (Andhra Pradesh, Karnataka, Maha-rashtra, and Tamil Nadu). Such situations undoubtedly exist in all parts of India, although likely at lower density in some of the northern states (see box 6.1). In most areas where such concentrations of high-risk subpopulations exist, the HIV prevalence among prenatal clinic patients has not progressed beyond 1 or 2 percent, despite the absence of extensive prevention programs and services until recently in many of those locations. This apparent constraint in epidemic growth suggests that in most areas, the prevailing sexual behaviors and networks are not sufficient to result in generalizing epidemics, the maintenance of which occurs independently of high-risk networks.

Nevertheless, the challenges and potential impact that this epidemic pattern poses should not be underestimated. The sheer size and complexity of India's population and the likely distribution of local concentrated epidemics across a large number of small urban areas and in certain rural settings pose major challenges. For example, the detailed mapping and assessments that were conducted in Karnataka have shown that in more than 250 small cities and towns, as well as in some rural areas in certain districts, large enough local female sex

---

Box 6.1 Declining HIV Prevalence in South India but Not in North India

Evidence has recently been presented suggesting that HIV prevalence may be declining in some southern Indian states, but not in north India (Kumar and others 2006). Unlinked, anonymous HIV prevalence data were analyzed from 294,050 women attending 216 prenatal clinics and 58,790 men attending 132 STI clinics from 2000 to 2004. Southern and northern states were analyzed separately. Kumar and colleagues reported that age-standardized HIV prevalence among women 15 to 24 years of age in south India fell significantly from 1.7 percent to 1.1 percent from 2000 to 2004. HIV prevalence in north India was found to be fivefold lower than in the south, but with no evidence of any declines from 2000 to 2004. HIV prevalence among south Indian STI clients 20 to 29 years of age also fell, but prevalence remained relatively stable among STI clients in north India. The authors concluded that the one-third decline in HIV prevalence among young women in south India was genuine and not caused by selection or testing biases or by mortality. The authors argued that the decline was not primarily caused by STI treatment because HIV prevalence fell even among young men with ulcerative and presumably viral STIs. They concluded that the declines in HIV prevalence among young women may be caused primarily by high levels of condom use in the context of commercial sex.

Source: Kumar and others 2006.

work networks can lead to substantial local HIV transmission (Swasti and KHPT 2004). In Bagalkot district of northern Karnataka, up to 50 percent of villages have at least 10 female SWs living and working in them. The widespread distribution of such high-risk pockets suggests that targeted interventions confined to large urban centers are insufficient to control this multitude of local epidemics and underscores the importance of well-focused rural programming.

In India, especially in rural areas and many parts of the north, the HIV epidemic appears relatively truncated and dependent primarily on men who migrate from rural areas to large urban centers. For example, in some districts in the Shekhawati area of northern Rajasthan, a detailed assessment has demonstrated that up to 50 percent of the households have at least one male who has migrated for work, usually to a large city, such as Mumbai in Maharashtra or Ahmedabad or Surat in Gujarat (Adrien and others 2005). Despite this large-scale migration and evidence that a substantial proportion of these men are sex clients at the destinations of migration, the adult HIV prevalence in this region has not surpassed 1 percent. The evidence suggests that although little female sex work exists at the villages of origin, men commonly have multiple sexual partners. In the absence of local high-risk networks to amplify transmission, these local epidemics will remain truncated because they depend on bridging from a distal high-risk network. Because many of these migrants spend relatively long periods away from home, they have less sexual contact with their regular partners in the village of origin. Moreover, this pattern of long-term migration decreases the likelihood of concurrent sexual relationships, which further reduces the risk of HIV transmission to regular partners, at least in the short term.

Few places in India are likely to experience truly generalizing epidemics, but a substantial number of individuals in the general population who do not belong to defined high-risk groups may still be infected with HIV—as is already the case in some high prevalence areas. HIV acquisition in most such circumstances, however, is highly dependent on connections to high-risk sexual or IDU networks, or both. It is likely that the conditions for a more generalized pattern of epidemic spread exist in some of the high-prevalence districts of Maharashtra, Karnataka, and Andhra Pradesh; they could occur in rural areas, perhaps more so than urban areas, because HIV prevalence in rural areas is often higher than in urban areas in high-prevalence districts. As noted previously, a population-based survey in Bagalkot district of northern Karnataka showed a significantly higher HIV prevalence in rural villages than in urban centers, with the HIV prevalence reaching as high as 8 percent in one of the villages (ICHAP 2004). Behavioral surveys in those areas have found that relatively high proportions of both men and women reported noncommercial casual sexual partners.

Special Considerations with Respect to HIV Transmission Dynamics

The size and complexity of India's HIV/AIDS epidemic give rise to a number of important issues that require particular attention, such as the mobility of sex workers and clients, the dynamics of rural epidemics, men having sex with men, injecting drug use and sex work and the availability of antiretroviral therapy.

Mobility of Sex Workers and Clients   A high proportion of female SWs in India move, often as frequently as every two weeks. In major cities with large female SW subpopulations, such as Mumbai, many of these women come from other parts of India or outside of the country. Even in smaller urban centers, many female SWs are mobile. The mobility of female SWs can contribute to HIV transmission by connecting high-risk sexual networks and thereby increasing HIV prevalence in those subpopulations. Frequent oscillating migration may increase exposure to people with acute HIV infection, who have increased viral load and HIV infectivity. In contrast, long-term migration may trap HIV within relationships, by limiting the geographic areas and people exposed to HIV during acute infection periods. In many areas, clients of female SWs are also highly mobile, within districts as well as within and between states, increasing the pace at which high-risk networks are linked, and this pattern can amplify local epidemics.

Rural Epidemics   Approximately 60 to 70 percent of Indians live in rural areas, and growing evidence suggests that the HIV epidemic is as advanced in some rural areas, particularly in southern and northeastern states, as it is in urban areas. Although some rural epidemics likely depend on urban transmission, evidence from many high-prevalence areas suggests the independence of rural epidemics and highlights a need to address them directly. As discussed previously, it seems that most rural epidemics are driven by commercial sex work (and injecting drug use in the northeast), although some pockets may have the conditions for generalizing epidemics.

Men Having Sex with Men   Recent evidence from prevention programs in several southern states indicates that the size and risk profile of MSM and *hijra* subpopulations have been underestimated in much of India. Although the size of these high-risk subpopulations is higher in large urban areas than previously estimated, emerging evidence also reveals sizable MSM and *hijra* communities in many smaller cities and towns. In many locations, MSM have both commercial and noncommercial sexual partners, thus forming important links between high-risk MSM and heterosexual networks.

Injecting Drug Use and Sex Work   With the rapid expansion of the HIV epidemic among IDUs in northeastern states, a growing number of women, many of them widows of men who have died from HIV/AIDS, engage in sex work. This emerging pattern will likely amplify the epidemic and require a more comprehensive prevention strategy.

Availability of Antiretroviral Therapy   Antiretroviral therapy (ART) is already widely available in the marketplace through private, informal systems. Many private doctors and untrained providers are prescribing inappropriate regimens. In addition, a government-sponsored program offers ART in some public health facilities. The generally low level of knowledge about HIV, coupled with the apparent availability of ART, could result in behavioral disinhibition, although no strong data support this notion in India. Conversely, increasing access to ART may motivate more people to seek counseling and testing, which may reinforce prevention efforts.

India's Response

The National AIDS Control Organization coordinates the government's overall HIV/AIDS response. The first phase of the National AIDS Control Program was initiated in 1992 as the first comprehensive national agenda of HIV/AIDS activities. It was also the first World Bank–financed HIV/AIDS project in the region and the second globally. (Appendix A lists World Bank–supported HIV/AIDS programs and activities in South Asia to date.) The first phase of the National AIDS Control Program focused largely on increasing general awareness about HIV, initiating preventive interventions in high-risk groups in large urban areas, improving blood safety, strengthening services for sexually transmitted infections (STIs), and monitoring the epidemic. A second phase launched in 1999 emphasized decentralization, with more functions delegated to the State AIDS Control Societies, which were created specifically to implement the activities under the program. Affiliated with state governments, project directors and other key officers of State AIDS Control Societies are generally government officials. The second phase of the National AIDS Control Program focused on the following strategic areas:

• Strengthening surveillance, through sentinel HIV surveillance, improved case reporting, mapping, and behavioral surveillance

• Scaling up targeted interventions with high-risk populations and improving STI management and condom programming

• Encouraging prevention in the general population through information, education, and communication (IEC) and special public education initiatives; improved blood safety; and scaled-up voluntary counseling and testing

• Expanding care and support services (primarily through community-based care centers), improving management of opportunistic infections, and preventing mother to child transmission

• Enhancing the enabling environment and reducing stigma and discrimination.

The World Bank retained its role as the principal financier of National AIDS Control Program, but the second phase received substantial funding to support specific components of HIV prevention, care, and support from bilateral donors—mainly the Canadian International Development Agency, U.K. Department for International Development (DFID), and U.S. Agency for International Development (USAID)—as well as private foundations—chiefly the Bill & Melinda Gates Foundation through the *Avahan* India AIDS Initiative.

This analysis of the programmatic response in India focuses on the status of the implementation of targeted interventions. This strategy has been a cornerstone of the second phase of program for high-risk groups, including female SWs, IDUs, MSM, truckers, migrant men, and street children. (Appendix B defines the various prevention intervention packages for targeted approaches.) This analysis of the epidemic in India indicates that an emphasis on targeted interventions is the right strategy. However, the pace and approach of scaling up these interventions (that is, high-impact interventions, specifically tailored to the needs of groups at high risk) require adjustment to interrupt the expansion of the myriad concentrated epidemics across India. Furthermore, reaching the marginalized and often hidden high-risk groups requires an enabling sociolegal environment. Specific issues related to the following areas bear particular consideration:

- enabling environment

- scaling up of efforts to increase coverage of high-impact interventions

- critical gaps.

Enabling Environment   Actively debated at present in India, reforms of existing laws and policies will enhance the rights of marginalized communities, including people living with HIV and AIDS, SWs, MSM, and IDUs, and will provide a powerful impetus to increase the scope, quality, and effectiveness of HIV responses.

Another impetus to improve the delivery and use of prevention, care, support, and treatment services of sufficient scope and quality stems from the reduction of stigma and discrimination among the general population and the creation of supportive social settings by decision makers, health workers, and educators. Multisectoral involvement can contribute to this cause by the development of an effective communication strategy, raising awareness early in schools and higher educational institutions, and promoting workplace interventions through appropriate programs and services.

Scaling Up of High-Impact Interventions   Overall coverage of high-risk networks with targeted interventions is insufficient. As figure 6.12 for South and Southeast Asia shows, coverage of SWs is below 20 percent, coverage of IDUs is below 5 percent, and coverage of MSM is below 1 percent (Policy Project 2004).

Figure 6.12 Coverage of High-Risk Groups in South and Southeast Asia, 2004

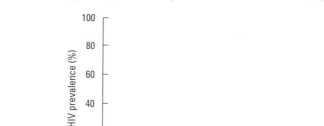

Source: Policy Project 2004.

The National AIDS Control Organization is supporting 835 targeted interventions; Andhra Pradesh has the highest number of such interventions (96) among all states. Only 199 (24 percent) of all targeted interventions focus on female SWs, 24 (less than 3 percent) on MSM, and 63 (7.5 percent) on IDUs. Projects supported by bilateral donors and private foundations also include targeted interventions for these high-risk groups, but coverage needs to increase substantially. For example, in Karnataka alone, a detailed mapping exercise identified more than 250 cities and towns with an approximate average of 100 female SWs at each location (Swasti and KHPT 2004). Given the emerging evidence of fairly widespread high-risk MSM networks, a substantial expansion of targeted interventions should cover that group, too.

Currently, almost half of all targeted interventions (48 percent) focus on migrant workers and truckers, presuming that those male populations constitute important bridge populations. A more rational approach would entail a greater focus on SWs and their clients, whoever they might be, at sex work locations. A focus on truckers is relevant because they can be reached efficiently and are obvious bridges between different sex work networks. However, the current strategy for trucker interventions is somewhat piecemeal, focusing on a few large truck-halt points rather than mapping out locations of large sex work operations.

Nongovernmental organizations (NGOs) implement most targeted interventions, but the content and quality of interventions vary by

NGO. (Appendix B shows the high-impact interventions most likely to have the largest effect if they reach high coverage levels through well-targeted and sustained efforts.) In some states that are supported by bilateral projects, NGOs receive capacity building and supportive supervision to implement targeted and tailored interventions. In other states without such support, the state AIDS control societies assume that responsibility, but most have only one staff member (the NGO adviser) to manage all NGOs implementing not only targeted prevention interventions but also care and support activities. Moreover, the dearth of well-articulated strategies, resources, and tools limits guidance for NGOs in implementing targeted interventions. Building capacity at state government and NGO levels is critical to supporting NGO-managed prevention programs. In addition, vulnerable communities—including female SW, MSM and IDU communities—must be mobilized and empowered to support and take on prevention programming.

Although all targeted interventions should include STI services as a component, NGOs generally face challenges in implementing and promoting high-quality STI services, including functional referral, as part of their projects. As a result, many members of high-risk groups (for example, female SWs, their clients, MSM, and IDUs) do not have access to adequate STI services.

Critical Gaps Several critical gaps exist:

- *Rural programs.* To date, almost all prevention programs have focused on urban populations, but the epidemic is just as advanced, if not more so, in many rural areas. Little is known about these rural epidemics, but in the many locations in Rajasthan and Karnataka where we have examined the situation closely, local sex work plays an important part in HIV transmission dynamics. Developing a strategy for focused prevention in rural areas should therefore be a priority.

- *Mobile populations.* High proportions of SWs and their clients move within districts, between districts, and between states. This mobility likely has epidemiological significance because sex workers and clients moving between areas with differential HIV prevalence could hasten the expansion of the epidemic. Moreover, programming for mobile SWs presents tactical challenges, given the difficulty of maintaining continuous outreach and peer education, condom supplies, and STI services.

- *MSM and IDU programs.* Few targeted interventions focus on MSM and IDUs (outside of the northeast), and NGOs face challenges in project design and implementation that lower intervention coverage and quality for these groups in most locations. A concerted effort is required to develop strategies involving peer education and implementation capabilities for rapid expansion of interventions targeting MSM and IDUs.

Major Achievements

Notwithstanding those challenges, India has made major strides and recorded notable successes in its response to the HIV epidemic. Nationally, the epidemic has slowed and may be stabilizing. In a state with one of the earliest and most severe epidemics in India, Tamil Nadu, several indicators point to encouraging trends—often referred to as an Asian success story—although major challenges remain (see box 6.1). As shown in figure 6.13, HIV prevalence seems to have stabilized among the general population (as estimated by prenatal clinic patients), STI clients, and MSM; however, HIV prevalence continues to climb among IDUs, reflecting inadequate recognition and programming for this high-risk group (NACO 2005).

Data from at least nine rounds of state-specific behavioral surveillance surveys suggest a stabilization of Tamil Nadu's HIV epidemic. For example, as figure 6.14 shows, condom use has risen to very high levels among all clients of female SWs, including regular ones, and has increased modestly among regular partners of FSWs (APAC 2004).

Figure 6.13 HIV Trends in Tamil Nadu, 1998–2003

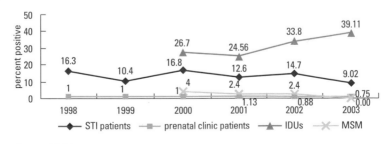

Source: NACO 2005.

Figure 6.14 Condom Use among Clients and Sex Partners of Female SWs in Tamil Nadu, India, 1996–2004

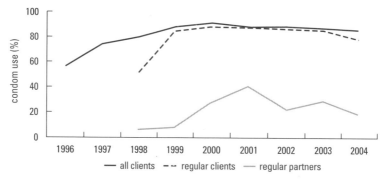

Source: APAC 2004.

In addition to the progress in Tamil Nadu, the Sonagachi Project in West Bengal has inspired many sex worker programs within India and globally. Box 6.2 describes this project in greater detail (Gangopadhyay, Chanda, and Sarkar 2005; U.S. Bureau of the Census 2006).

Nepal

Epidemic Overview

Nepal appears to have the potential for a substantial epidemic, at least among high-risk groups, especially female SWs and IDUs. Injecting drug use occurs across the country and significantly overlaps with commercial sex. A high number of women migrate or are trafficked to work as female SWs in India, especially Mumbai. Those returning to Nepal from Mumbai have much higher HIV prevalence than those who have remained in the country, so migration and trafficking to and from Mumbai can rapidly increase HIV prevalence in Nepali SW networks. As with other South Asian countries, injecting drug use, as well as female and male sex work, is likely to continue to drive the HIV epidemic in Nepal, particularly in light of the nexus between injecting drug use and sex work.

Nepal's Response

The National AIDS Control Program was established in Nepal in 1988, after the first cases of AIDS were reported. Four years later, the

Box 6.2 The Sonagachi Project, West Bengal, India

The Sonagachi Project works with about 6,000 SWs who serve approximately half a million clients annually in Sonagachi, Kolkata's major red-light district. The project promotes a comprehensive approach to HIV prevention, encompassing contextual reform through improved policing practices, solidarity and community empowerment, improved sexual and reproductive health care, child care, peer education and out-reach, and condom promotion. The project, which is cited as a model of social change and community empowerment, has several impressive achievements, as illustrated in the figure below. These achievements include the following:

- Increasing condom use in sex work, from 3 percent in 1992, to 70 percent in 1994, to 90 percent in 1998. By 1998, these proportions were far higher than those observed in surrounding red-light areas.
- Reducing STI rates among SWs, by over 75 percent. Syphilis and genital ulcer cases fell from 28 percent and 7 percent, respectively, in 1992, to 11 percent and 2 percent in 1998.
- Stabilizing HIV prevalence among SWs, at 1 to 2 percent in 1992 and 1994. In 1996, HIV prevalence rose to 11 percent and remained at that level in 1997. HIV prevalence among SWs elsewhere in India has generally increased more steeply.

Achievements of the Sonagachi Project

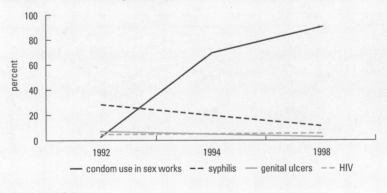

Source: UNAIDS 2002.

National AIDS Coordination Committee (NACC) was formed. Chaired by the minister of health, NACC is a multisectoral body providing overall policy guidance with representatives from other line ministries, United Nations (UN) agencies, NGOs, civil society groups, and other stakeholders. To implement the National Policy for HIV Prevention and other related activities, the National Center for

AIDS and Sexually Transmitted Disease Control (NCASC) was established in 1995 and reports to NACC, advising it on technical issues. NCASC consists of a director, deputy director, medical and public health officers, and consultants. More recently, the National AIDS Council (NAC) was established, with the prime minister as the chair, to raise the profile of HIV/AIDS issues. NACC now reports to the NAC. At the district level, district development committees implement and monitor HIV/AIDS projects according to national strategies and guidelines. They report to the NCASC. Surveillance of HIV, STIs, and behavior in Nepal has been neither systematic nor continuous, because of political instability and other reasons. Much of available HIV prevalence data derive from clients of voluntary counseling and testing (VCT) centers, which have very limited coverage and capacity and are probably biased toward clients who undergo diagnostic testing. Limited surveillance on STI patients and cross-sectional studies on high-risk groups provide additional biobehavioral data.

In 2000, the NCASC commissioned a situation and response analysis, which recommended developing a clearer national strategy, increasing political commitment, strengthening technical and management capacity, decreasing frequent staff turnover, increasing program coverage among high-risk groups, and providing care and support for people living with HIV and AIDS (PLWHAs). A new national HIV prevention strategy was developed for 2002–6, with a budget of about US$50 million, of which the Global Fund to Fight AIDS, Tuberculosis, and Malaria (GFATM) was expected to contribute about 20 percent. Priority areas include expanded HIV and STI prevention among high-risk groups and young people; accessible care and support services for PLWHAs; enhanced surveillance, monitoring, and evaluation; and more effective and efficient management. The Nepal Initiative was launched by the following partners to carry out this national strategy: the government of Nepal, the Joint United Nations Programme on HIV/AIDS (UNAIDS), the United Nations Development Programme (UNDP), the Australian Agency for International Development (AusAID), DFID, and USAID.

Although the Nepal Initiative ended in 2003, external agencies continue to coordinate their efforts through the Expanded UN Theme Group. Projects have been launched in this manner on behavior-change communication, condom promotion, condom social marketing, and mass media awareness. Plans are in place to expand prevention programs for migrants and youth, as well as care and support services for PLWHAs through the GFATM. However, little of the overall plan has actually been implemented, largely because of Nepal's political instability. Nepal currently has nine VCT centers, three run by the government and six by NGOs, but further efforts are needed to expand those centers in scope and coverage.

NCASC is currently reviewing its surveillance strategy and intends to launch second-generation surveillance among STI patients, tuberculosis patients, military personnel, prenatal clinic patients, and blood donors. Whether those plans include female SWs, IDUs, and migrants remains unclear. Because different organizations have assumed responsibility for surveillance and prevention on a project basis, a coherent, comprehensive perspective of the epidemic across the country is difficult to ascertain, and little documented evaluation of these projects' effects has been undertaken. Although the HIV epidemic in Nepal seems somewhat more advanced than that in Bangladesh or Pakistan, similar priorities apply—such as an urgent need to increase targeted interventions for female SWs, MSM, and IDUs, in particular. Interventions for female SWs should place a special emphasis on those who have migrated or plan to migrate to India. In 2004, the World Bank sponsored a cost-effectiveness study for NCASC to assist policy makers in making budgetary decisions for different kinds of HIV prevention interventions. According to that study, funding for interventions directed toward high-risk groups made up approximately 50 percent of the overall budget, but only 6 percent went toward harm reduction for IDUs. Over 30 percent of the budget was spent on more general population interventions, including those for youth, which did not feature among the top five cost-effective interventions.

Strategic investments on prevention programs among female SWs, IDUs, and perhaps MSM could have a major effect in curtailing the growth of the HIV epidemic in Nepal. Notwithstanding the rapid epidemic growth initially observed among IDUs in Nepal, evidence suggests that interventions, particularly those mounted by NGOs, have reduced risky injecting and sexual behaviors and curtailed HIV transmission among those reached. For example, a harm reduction program providing education and safe injecting equipment to IDUs in Kathmandu increased knowledge, reduced unsafe injection practices tenfold, and stabilized HIV prevalence at 1.6 percent (Peak and others 1995). Box 6.3 outlines further steps toward a stronger institutional response to HIV/AIDS.

Pakistan

Epidemic Overview

The HIV epidemic in Pakistan remains at an early stage. Growing evidence based on available data from several of the larger cities sug-

---

Box 6.3   Steps toward a Stronger Institutional Response to HIV/AIDS in Nepal

Nepal has all the risk factors for a potentially explosive and generalized HIV epidemic: relatively high prevalence rates among female SWs and MSM, very high rates among IDUs in certain urban locations, and significant evidence for higher HIV rates among migrant laborers, especially those returning from India.

In the past several years, Nepal's response to the HIV/AIDS challenge has been characterized by a sound strategy, strong planning, and substantial resources—but subdued implementation (with the exception of USAID-financed activities, implemented through separate nongovernmental channels). The single most important impediment to a stronger, more effective response has been identified as the lack of an appropriate institutional mechanism with sufficient multisectoral partnership, civil society involvement, bureaucratic flexibility, authority, and capacity. The result has been weak implementation.

A large proportion of committed resources (from GFATM and more recently from DFID) has remained unspent for long periods of time, despite the existence of several nongovernmental and community-based organizations working on HIV/AIDS that are ready to scale up effective interventions if more resources can be channeled to them. A need therefore exists to build a bridge between available unspent resources (at the central level) and available unused capacity (at the grassroots level).

An Institutional Task Force was set up in May 2005 to assess the institutional mechanisms in place to address HIV and AIDS in Nepal and to recommend improvements. The task force met regularly to review available literature and background documentation (including a draft HIV/AIDS bill that was proposed last year) and consulted with stakeholders, producing several optional models for the Nepal HIV/AIDS program. The task force also benefited from a capacity assessment that was commissioned jointly by USAID and the World Bank and contracted through Family Health International with the specific objective of informing the task force's work.

On the basis of the task force's work, a draft Institutional Options Paper was prepared (November 2005). The paper identifies the main institutional issues:

Box 6.3 *(continued)*

- capacity constraints—in the government and nongovernmental sectors
- lack of sufficient authority and procedural flexibility within the government system
- weak or nonfunctional intersectoral coordination mechanism
- inadequate public-private partnerships
- need for improvement in the donor coordination mechanisms.

Moreover, the paper outlines the following principles for selecting a stronger institutional mechanism for the HIV/AIDS program implementation:

- strong and equal partnership with civil society
- adequate level of autonomy and authority to make rules and procedures
- separation of the policy, coordination, and oversight functions of the board and the operational responsibilities of a unit or secretariat
- use of existing institutional structures.

Among the institutional options suggested by the paper in order to mount a truly effective intersectoral response is the establishment of a semiautonomous entity—with its own board and an operational and funding unit. Another option being considered is the use of an existing autonomous entity, such as the Poverty Alleviation Fund, to channel funds to community groups rapidly. The latter idea is proposed to be tested on a pilot basis.

Apart from the establishment of the Institutional Task Force and its work, progress has been made in getting GFATM- and DFID-financed activities off the ground through a management support agency contract with the UNDP. This arrangement is temporary, to be replaced by a more permanent institutional mechanism expected to emerge from the work of the task force. Also, the NGO networks have been making attempts to organize themselves more effectively, to be able to better absorb available donor funds and scale up HIV interventions targeted at vulnerable populations.

Source: World Bank staff.

gests that the substantial size and high-risk behaviors of IDUs, MSM, and female SWs could contribute to local concentrated epidemics.

At this time, efforts to curb HIV transmission in Pakistan should focus on IDU networks. Molecular epidemiological studies have found that viral isolates are very similar, suggesting the recent introduction of HIV into the country's IDU networks. Several cities have large, street-based IDU subpopulations, and rapid increases in HIV prevalence have been observed (for example, in Karachi and Larkana). The extent to which an IDU-driven epidemic will trigger epidemics in other subpopulations remains unclear, but injecting drug use overlaps with high-risk sexual networks of female SWs and their clients. Several cities also have relatively large populations of MSM, but more information is needed regarding their sexual risk behaviors and networking. Because much of the visible MSM activity seems commercialized, the potential for substantial HIV transmission in this subpopulation is high.

Cities such as Karachi, Lahore, and Multan have significant female SW subpopulations as well, but HIV transmission in that group has remained at a low level. As in the case of MSM, not enough is known about the organization of sex work and associated risk behaviors to predict the potential for rapid HIV spread. A few available studies have described brothel-based sex work, especially in Lahore, but most sex work seems dispersed. In Karachi, this dispersion appears to have increased in the past several years as female SWs from the red-light areas have moved to new locations. This shift could slow the pace of epidemic growth, but it also increases the difficulty of implementing interventions and delivering services.

Pakistan's Response

The Federal Committee on AIDS was established in 1987, with the national health secretary as the chair, to provide policy guidelines, develop strategic plans, and coordinate with international agencies and organizations. One year later, the National AIDS Control Program was formed as part of the National Institute of Health to serve as a resource center for national guidelines and protocols, as well as human resource development, covering surveillance, counseling, clinical management, care and support, and blood safety. Provincial AIDS control programs were formed in 1994 under the provincial departments of health. These programs are responsible for implementation of public education, blood safety, and education for clinical and laboratory personnel, among other activities. HIV surveillance sites have been established in 47 VCT centers, all public sector blood banks, and STI clinics in all public sector referral hospitals throughout the country. In addition, a comprehensive second-generation surveillance program is in the advanced planning stages, and behavioral data collection has been piloted in Karachi and Rawalpindi. The baseline behavioral surveillance survey among high-risk groups has been completed, and a survey among bridging and general population groups will begin in the medium and longer term. Despite those efforts, surveillance information from Pakistan needs further improvement. Case reporting has suffered from inadequate diagnostic skills, unreliable supplies of diagnostic kits and other inputs, and nonstandardized testing regimens. Most behavioral research has consisted of small-scale cross-sectional studies, conducted largely in urban health facilities, which do not reflect the situation countrywide.

Programmatic responses in Pakistan remained at a low level until after the government lifted a ban on the dissemination of HIV/AIDS-related information in 1993. A public education campaign followed, and in 2000, the National Strategic Framework for HIV/AIDS was developed through a broad consultative process and with UNAIDS support. An evaluation of the public education campaign in 2001 revealed major gaps in knowledge and awareness, and in 2003, the Enhanced HIV Control Program was established with funding from the World Bank, UN agencies, and bilateral donors. The program has the following components:

- expanded service delivery through public sector and NGO prevention programs targeting female SWs, IDUs, MSM, *hijras*, migrant workers, and prisoners

- education and communication programs targeting the general population

- blood safety

- technical and managerial capacity building

- care for PLWHAs.

However, shortages of qualified staff, persistent lack of technical and managerial expertise, and limited capacity of NGOs to deliver effective prevention services have delayed implementation of some program components.

Although IDU and female SW subpopulations exhibit high risk and vulnerability, the size of those groups and the extent of their risk and vulnerability remain largely unknown. Further mapping and enumeration activities need to be undertaken, particularly in the major urban centers, where injecting drug use and sex work appear to overlap.

Those activities should also provide evidence of risk behaviors and networks to inform the design and expansion of harm reduction for IDUs, as well as of appropriate HIV prevention for female SWs and MSM and their clients and partners. Increasing intervention coverage among those groups could curtail the development of a major HIV epidemic in Pakistan. Targeted interventions should place particular emphasis on female SWs who inject drugs, or whose partners inject drugs, in the large urban centers where such behavior seems prevalent.

Bangladesh

Epidemic Overview

In Bangladesh, the HIV epidemic also remains at an early phase, but high levels of mobility may exacerbate HIV vulnerability. As elsewhere in the region, the HIV epidemic appears unlikely to generalize beyond dependency on high-risk networks, particularly SW networks. The large cities, however, have relatively large subpopulations of brothel- and lodge-based female SWs who have a high client volume, indicating the potential for substantial concentrated epidemics. The distribution of female sex work beyond Dhaka and other cities remains largely unknown, making assessment of the epidemic potential problematic. Some evidence suggests that the HIV epidemic could expand, at least locally, because of injecting drug use. A transition from smoking drugs to injecting drugs could result in relatively large numbers of IDUs, and the intersection between female SW and IDU networks could lead to a rapid expansion of the HIV epidemic if HIV prevention efforts are not intensified. Bangladesh's epidemic potential also features a potentially important overlap between female SW and MSM networks, but more data are required to substantiate this observation.

Bangladesh's Response

The National AIDS Committee, chaired by the minister of health and family welfare, was formed in October 1985 and includes secretaries from other line ministries, members of parliament, and representatives from NGOs and other civil society groups. The National AIDS Committee serves as a central advisory body to the government on all

HIV/AIDS- and STI-related issues, including program and financial management, ethical, and legal issues. Three subcommittees report to the committee, including a technical subcommittee composed of HIV/AIDS and STI prevention and control specialists. The Ministry of Health and Family Welfare (MOHFW) is designated as the coordinating and executive body for HIV/AIDS- and STI-related activities. Under the MOHFW, the Directorate General of Health Services created the National AIDS and Sexually Transmitted Disease Programme (NASP) as part of its Health and Population Sector Programme in 1998. A line directorship for the NASP was established, which would accelerate program implementation and to raise the profile of the government's HIV/AIDS response. Staff members reporting to this line director include a program manager, deputy program managers, and technical consultants.

In 1998, NASP activities included education for the health sector and general population as well as targeted interventions for vulnerable groups. The World Bank, DFID, and USAID have provided financial support, but funding was halved after a midterm review documented a slow implementation rate. Three UN agencies—the United Nations Children's Fund (UNICEF), the United Nations Fund for Population Activities (UNFPA), and the World Health Organization (WHO)—have also provided technical assistance in NGO programming, advocacy and communication, condom procurement, VCT services, STI control, and blood safety services, among others. Although the MOHFW and NASP have gradually built political will and elevated leadership commitment, they need to enhance program development and implementation at local levels. Furthermore, NASP requires more stability in key personnel and coordinated management support to pursue such improvements. NASP has established a second-generation surveillance system to enable data collection for analysis of the HIV/STI situation and for identification of high-risk groups, but it needs to expand coverage to include both urban hotspots and key rural areas. NASP also needs to improve its monitoring and evaluation system with more sensitive and program-specific indicators and procedures for the effective flow of information and for the strategic use of information to alter program design.

Targeted interventions for high-risk groups are critical for Bangladesh in responding to the HIV epidemic, and NASP explicitly prioritizes four such groups for these interventions: female SWs, MSM, IDUs, and migrants.

Some interventions have been developed for female SWs, IDUs, and truck drivers—notably the Shakti project developed in cooperation with CARE Bangladesh. Because of a lack of proper enumeration studies, overall coverage remains unclear, but it is probably quite low. NASP and its implementing partners therefore need to conduct comprehensive mapping and enumeration studies that geographically and numerically define the subpopulations for interventions to reach and expand coverage to meet prevention needs. In particular, coverage of targeted interventions for female SWs needs to expand beyond those based in brothels (the focus of many current interventions), and STI services for female SWs and their clients need to be enhanced. NASP should also expand VCT services across the country.

With levels of HIV infection low both in the general population and still to a large extent in high-risk groups, but with levels of STIs high in high-risk groups, Bangladesh has a window of opportunity to saturate prevention program coverage, particularly among female SWs and also among MSM and IDUs, wherever the latter subpopulations are identified. Similar to the approach in Pakistan, prevention activities in Bangladesh should place a particular emphasis on female SWs who inject drugs or whose partners inject drugs to curtail an impending HIV epidemic.

Evidence from the Shakti project of CARE Bangladesh suggests that harm reduction can work. That project reaches an estimated 5,000 IDUs in Dhaka, providing them with a drop-in center, detoxification services, HIV prevention education and individual counseling, and safe injecting equipment. A recent evaluation (Tasnim, Hussein, and Kelly 2005) showed that, among IDUs, HIV prevalence has remained relatively low and sexual risk practices have declined. However, needle sharing has fluctuated, climbing from 66 percent in 2002 to 86 percent in 2004. Fieldworkers attribute this increase during the two-year period to police action against those carrying injecting equipment, which underscores the importance of legal reform to support harm reduction.

Sri Lanka

Epidemic Overview

Sri Lanka faces an HIV epidemic at an early phase, with limited potential for growth unless behavioral patterns change (for example, predominant modes of drug use shift from inhalation to injection) and HIV spreads within and across networks of high-risk groups (such as IDUs and female SWs). Structural factors may have contributed to the low prevalence in Sri Lanka, where even among female SWs, HIV prevalence has remained low. According to sentinel surveillance conducted from 1993 to 2004, of 13,533 serum samples collected from female SWs, only 11 tested positive; of 31,904 serum samples collected from STI patients (many of whom constitute the clientele of female SWs), only 31 tested positive. In 2003, the surveillance system began to draw serum samples from military service personnel and transportation workers, who may also be clients of female SWs, but none have tested positive yet. As expected with these findings, few serum samples obtained from the three other lower-risk groups that the surveillance system has covered since 1993 (tuberculosis patients, blood donors, and pregnant women) have tested positive. The 2005 round of sentinel surveillance included IDUs and MSM, and will generate baseline serological data for those groups.

In the absence of longitudinal behavioral surveillance data, findings from cross-sectional studies present a mixed profile of Sri Lanka's HIV-related behavioral patterns. One set of studies on drug use highlights inhalation through sniffing or smoking as the predominant mode of intake; however, if an increasing proportion of drug users were to start injecting, the epidemic could grow quickly. Hence, at minimum, the surveillance system should build in a mechanism to monitor modes of drug use. Another set of studies has revealed high STI prevalence and risky sexual behaviors (for example, multiple sexual partners and low condom use) that may predispose female SWs and MSM to HIV infection.

Sri Lanka's Response

In 1985, the Ministry of Health incorporated HIV prevention and control as part of the mandate of the National Sexually Transmitted Disease Control Programme (established in 1951) after it received an alert about India's first case of AIDS. The next year, the director general of health services launched and chaired the National Task Force for the Prevention and Control of HIV/AIDS, with representatives from the Ministry of Health, the Ceylon Tourist Board, and the police. By April 1987, Sri Lanka detected the first HIV cases among foreign visitors and its own population. Three months later, WHO assisted in developing a short-term plan of action comprising baseline serological surveys, as well as knowledge, attitude, and behavioral surveys. WHO began to finance the implementation of this plan of action at the beginning of 1988.

At about the same time, the Ministry of Health expanded the National Task Force to include representatives from other state sectors and renamed it the National AIDS Committee. With WHO's technical assistance during 1988, the ministry developed the first set of medium-term plans (MTP 1) for STI service enhancements as well as for HIV prevention and control. One year later, the Committee of Secretaries (a national-level executive body of presidentially appointed leaders that reports to ministers but runs the operations of their line ministries) approved the MTP 1 for HIV prevention and control. In 1991, the government, UNDP, and WHO signed an agreement to finance and implement the MTP 1, for which the government and UNDP would offer funding and WHO would continue to provide technical assistance. The MTP 1 reinforced the HIV prevention and control role of the National Sexually Transmitted Disease Control Programme. Renamed the National Sexually Transmitted Disease and AIDS Control Programme (NSACP), it began in 1992 to distribute condoms in its own network of STI clinics and in health care facilities, through partnerships with provincial health authorities. Additionally, brothels and massage parlors in the Colombo municipal area, as well as the armed forces, started to receive condom supplies. As part of the MTP 1, mapping was done of risk behaviors and the second round of knowledge, attitude, and behavioral surveys was conducted. The Ministry of Health's Health Education Bureau developed an operational plan for systematic IEC activities.

In 1994, the Ministry of Health developed the second set of medium-term plans (MTP 2) for HIV prevention and control for joint funding and implementation by the government and several UN agencies. In 1995, the government convened the Theme Group on HIV/AIDS, with representatives from the UN agencies operating in Sri Lanka to coordinate relevant activities. By 1997, the low disbursement rate of the secretariat grant prompted the recruitment of a country program adviser who would chair the Theme Group and liaise between it and NSACP. In 2000, a six-member team with representatives from the Ministry of Finance's Department of External Resources, the University of Colombo, UNAIDS, and WHO conducted an external review of MTP 2. The team noted that in accordance with recommendations from the MTP 1 review, NSACP had adopted a case definition for HIV/AIDS and initiated sentinel facility–based serological surveillance among female SWs, STI and tuberculosis patients, and pregnant women. The team acknowledged accomplishments of the multisectoral response in terms of IEC interventions for vulnerable (but not necessarily high-risk) subpopulations: youth, migrant workers, and tourism sector workers. The team reiterated, however, the need for the following:

- building in a mechanism to track patterns of drug use

- focusing HIV prevention on high-risk groups

- sustaining condom supplies and assessing recent social marketing initiatives

- expanding syndromic STI management.

Indeed, those shortcomings underscore the importance of a more comprehensive response, which could include, among other strategies, the following:

- second-generation surveillance, integrating serological and behavioral data collection, analysis, and use

- decreased legal and sociocultural barriers in reaching (for surveillance and intervention purposes) female SWs, their clients, MSM, IDUs, and other groups whose behaviors increase their HIV risk in addition to their social vulnerability

- institutional reforms with greater commitment, as well as fiscal, managerial, and technical decentralization to the provincial and district levels.

Those strategies constitute the basis of the government's current National Strategic Plan for HIV/AIDS Prevention and Control. Leveraging the support from some UN agencies, the World Bank has built on the STI and HIV control component of the Health Services Development Project with a US$12.55 million grant for the National HIV/AIDS Prevention Project. In 2004, one and a half years into its implementation, the project was confronted with serious bottlenecks and slow progress. To achieve measurable results, the government launched the Rapid Results Initiative to jump-start implementation and infuse enthusiasm and confidence into the program, as described in box 6.4.

Afghanistan

HIV-related data from Afghanistan are very sparse and largely limited to highly incomplete case reports. Nevertheless, Afghanistan is the world's largest opium producer (UNODC 2005b). Increased production and prolonged war and suffering have inevitably led to increased drug use. Hashish is commonplace and relatively socially acceptable; opium use is widespread in urban and rural areas. Although high-quality heroin is exported, adulterated heroin is available and used locally. It was historically smoked, but drug injection is increasing, introduced initially by Afghan refugees living in Iran and Pakistan. An estimated 15 to 25 percent of Afghan men consume hashish, 2 percent use opium, and 1 percent may use heroin (UNODC 2005b). A recent survey found that 4 percent of IDUs tested positive for HIV at a VCT center in Kabul (personal communication, Ministry of Public Health, Kabul, March 2006). Moreover, all of Afghanistan's neighbors (except Turkmenistan, for which no data are available) have significant concentrated HIV and hepatitis C epidemics among IDUs.

The Ministry of Public Health (MOPH) has developed a national strategic plan for Afghanistan for the period from 2003 to 2007

Box 6.4   Sri Lanka Rapid Results Initiative to Jump-Start Implementation of HIV/AIDS Prevention Project

In 2004, one and a half years into implementation of a World Bank–supported HIV/AIDS prevention project, the project was confronted with serious bottlenecks and slow progress. The key impediments to implementation included turf issues between various teams in the Ministry of Health, limited accountability, and lack of a sense of urgency. In addition, the bureaucratic problems led to demotivation and demoralization of staff members, who lost sight of the program goals.

An urgent need existed to inject enthusiasm and confidence, so the National Sexually Transmitted Disease and AIDS Control Programme launched a Rapid Results Initiative in September 2004. The rapid results approach aims at jump-starting major change efforts and enhancing implementation capacity by creating 100-day result-producing "projects." This approach helps accelerate the achievement of longer-term objectives by focusing on specific, short-term, results-based goals that require the cooperation and collaboration of multiple stakeholders. The approach is based on strengthening

- capacity of leaders to challenge and to motivate
- local empowerment and accountability
- capacity for cross-institutional collaboration.

Implementation of the Rapid Results Initiative involves the following:

- focused challenge from high level to frontline staff
- creation of new alliances and partnerships to form teams at the front line
- empowered teams that refine challenge into concrete measurable goals and develop their own solutions (translated into action plans with clear roles and responsibilities, milestones, and budget)
- resources (financial and human) that are mobilized and managed by the teams to meet the challenge
- ownership of the challenge and goal by senior officials and the frontline staff, thereby fueling commitment and accountability
- opportunity for the frontline staff to demonstrate capabilities, take credit for success, and be recognized.

By December 2004, the Sri Lankan team had launched comprehensive care and treatment for 23 people living with HIV/AIDS, increased voluntary blood donation from 82 percent to 92 percent in Colombo and from 60 percent to 73 percent in Kandu, achieved the highest ever cure rate of new smear-positive tuberculosis patients in Colombo, and increased consistent condom use among field SWs in Colombo from less than 10 percent to more than 25 percent.

Source: World Bank staff.

(MOPH 2003). The plan is being revised through a broad-based partic-
ipatory process, with thematic working groups addressing these issues:

- capacity development and leadership (institutional development,
  multisector approaches, surveillance, monitoring, and evaluation)

- high-risk and vulnerable groups

- health sector issues (blood safety, VCT, links to tuberculosis and
  reproductive health, treatment, care and support)

- IEC.

These thematic groups, supported by a technical advisory group of
coordinating agencies, are developing the framework for an updated
national HIV/AIDS plan of action, covering management and technical support, capacity, and advocacy and mobilization activities. The
National AIDS Control Program consists of a small team (a manager
and focal personnel for blood safety, IEC, and surveillance) and a
demand reduction team are in place in the MOPH under the general
director of primary health care. The consultancies, technical assistance, and limited funding for the planning, programming, and implementation of various activities will benefit from improved interagency
coordination. Some joint activities are undertaken with the Ministry
of Counter Narcotics, under the umbrella of demand reduction, such
as a government-endorsed policy on harm reduction.

The 2006 national development strategy includes a five-year
benchmark for HIV/AIDS: to maintain a low prevalence of HIV-
positive cases (less than 0.5 percent) in the population to reduce
mortality and morbidity associated with HIV/AIDS. The MOPH
leadership views HIV/AIDS as a development issue, and the ministry
increasingly plays a leading role in steering, policy, and guidance,
when working with other sectors and ministries to enhance a multisectoral response and with NGOs to reach out to high-risk populations.
Initial efforts are under way to integrate HIV/AIDS services in the
government's basic package of health services, aiming to cover 90
percent of the population, but few NGOs are involved in HIV/AIDS
prevention and treatment.

Bhutan

A total of 74 cases have been detected in Bhutan through surveillance, medical screening (for people leaving the country for education and training purposes), contact tracing, blood donor screening, voluntary testing, and prenatal screening. The male-to-female ratio of the detected cases is about 1.2:1, representing diverse backgrounds—sex workers, businessmen, uniformed services, civil servants, and housewives. Bhutan's borders with India are extremely porous. Many of the locally acquired infections have occurred in Phuntsholing, a town across the border from West Bengal. Sex work—using Bhutanese, Indian, and Nepali women—exists on both sides of the border and is very fluid, but cross-border programmatic cooperation has been limited to date.

Internal and international migration occurs to a large extent. For example, civil servants travel inside and outside the country, including to India and Thailand, and have reported engaging in casual and commercial sex during their journeys. The Bhutan army trains in India in two high-prevalence states, Maharashtra and Tamil Nadu. Many Indian men migrate to Bhutan for work, including military personnel and construction and hydroelectric power laborers. An initial social assessment suggested limited interaction between those Indian populations and local communities, but that observation requires confirmation with further studies.

Bhutan has displayed remarkable openness at all levels, from the king to monks and district health workers. Political will and operational commitment are multisectoral and reach beyond the health sector to include defense and transportation, among other key sectors.

The Maldives

HIV-related data are very sparse and are largely limited to highly incomplete case reports (about 80 cases). In the Maldives, citizens working and traveling abroad comprised a significant number of the cases reported. Recent observational reports suggest considerable growth in injecting drug use.

CHAPTER 7

Scaling Up HIV Prevention Programs

A critical strategy for curtailing the HIV epidemic in the South Asia Region is to prevent further HIV transmission in areas with locally concentrated HIV epidemics that are driven by high-risk practices among networks involving sex workers (SWs), injecting drug users (IDUs) and men having sex with men (MSM). Unless focused prevention activities—sometimes called targeted interventions as in the National AIDS Control and Prevention program (NACP) in India—are taken to sufficient scale, the overall influence on the epidemic will be marginal. The heterogeneity and diversity of local epidemics in the region present a complex challenge for the planning and implementation of a scaled-up response. This chapter presents a general rubric for scaling up, that is, expanding coverage of, focused prevention programs.

Distribution of High-Risk Networks

For prevention programs to achieve high coverage of members of high-risk networks, the programs must consider both the geographic distribution and the size of the key population networks. For example, in circumstances in which large SW populations are highly concentrated geographically, high coverage can theoretically be achieved by placing programs and services in those locations. In contrast, if SWs are more widely distributed in smaller pockets, high coverage can only be achieved if a large proportion of the locations is covered, and this might require a more staggered approach.

Elements of Scaling up of Program Coverage

In circumstances in which many localized high-risk networks exist, expanding coverage of programs needs to be approached at both the geographic (that is, district) level and network (or hotspot) level. This approach is illustrated in figure 7.1.

First, increasing access at the district level is achieved by placing prevention programs and services in locations or hotspots that contain a high proportion of the key at-risk populations (for example, SWs or IDUs). District-level planning defines the upper limit of coverage. Second, within these identified networks or hotspots, coverage of services and programs represents the extent to which members of such high-risk networks or hotspots access and use preventive services and adopt behavior change. The ability of local programs to mobilize and reach local key populations will have a large influence on the effective coverage of focused prevention programs.

Tactics for Scaling Up Coverage

To achieve a high level of coverage at the district level and within each hotspot, a logical sequence can be followed.

Figure 7.1   Program Coverage at District (Macro) and Local (Micro) levels

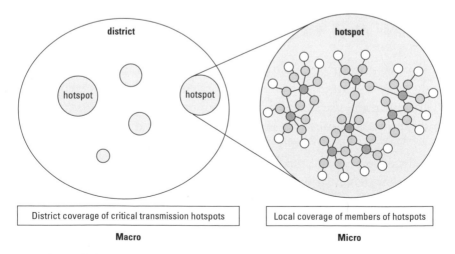

Source: Authors.

Step 1: Planning Comprehensive Geographic Mapping

The first step is to plan for high district-level coverage by identifying all of the key locations where high-risk networks exist. This approach includes a comprehensive mapping, which entails segmenting the geographic areas and identifying all of the specific locations and sites within those segments where members of high-risk networks congregate. This step can be accomplished using a structured approach to interviewing key informants. Local members of the high-risk population must be involved in this step of the process of site identification. A critical component of the mapping is an estimation of the size of the key populations at each location, and this is needed for realistic target setting.

Step 2: Situating Programs to Achieve High District-Level Coverage

Mapping provides information on the geographic distribution of the key populations and networks that need to be reached by focused prevention programs and services. This information can help guide the prioritization of locations where programs and services should be initiated. For example, a state or provincial program can decide to ensure that programs and services will be established in all cities, towns, and locations that contain at least 90 percent of the estimated high-risk populations, by a specified date. Setting such "targets" will help in planning and defining the configuration of programs. When key populations are highly concentrated, then programs can achieve a high level of coverage by focusing on a relatively small number of locations. In contrast, where key populations are geographically dispersed, programs and services might have to be phased in over time, with gradual expansion in coverage until full coverage is achieved.

Step 3: Planning Local Outreach and Services

Good coverage at the local network or hotspot level requires local planning of quality outreach and services. This planning involves specific segmentation of local key populations by locations and sites (such as a bus depot, train station, or cinema hall) and the operational characteristics of local key population members (for example, full-time versus part-time , street-based versus lodge-based, and day versus night sex work). Key population members, such as peer educators, must be involved in the assessment, planning, monitoring and outreach—this is critical to success and requires substantial capacity building and support.

General Considerations

Using a comprehensive approach to scale up focused prevention programs, as described in this section, requires that planners meet several conditions.

Condition 1: Flexible Strategies and Implementing Partnerships

The diverse distribution and characteristics of the key populations requires equally diversified strategies and partnerships for program implementation. Moreover, program planners must be able to be proactive in matching program resources to where the need is greatest, rather than being constrained and reactive to the distribution of potential implementing partners such as nongovernmental organizations (NGOs). This approach will often require more intensive support for local community-based organizations and NGOs, and sometimes the involvement of high-capacity implementers from other locations.

Condition 2: Strong Information-Gathering Systems

For organizations to effectively scale up outreach, they need strong systems to gather, analyze, and interpret information. The processes of mapping and performing local assessments and planning need to be fully integrated into the work program, roles and responsibilities of program planners, and must involve key stakeholders.

Condition 3: Local Planning Processes

Because planning needs to be detailed, it must be done at the local level. For example, the determination of where programs and services should be located should be done at the district level, rather than at the state or provincial levels. This process requires specific local information and investment in local analysis and planning. Local stakeholders must be involved in the program design.

Condition 4: Capacity Building

The demands of scaling up will not be met without extensive capacity building at all levels. In particular, systems are required to build capacity for technical support to local programs and to maintain that support.

CHAPTER 8

Summary of Recommendations

South Asia is facing an HIV epidemic that is severe in magnitude and scope, with an estimated 5.5 to 6 million people currently infected. At least 60 percent of HIV-positive people in Asia live in India alone. The epidemic is heterogeneous and diverse, requiring well informed, prioritized, and effective responses. On the basis of the evidence presented in this report, a number of recommendations are made for improving the quality and scope of HIV prevention programming and building the necessary capacity to do so. Expanding surveillance, mapping, and research to better understand the socioeconomic factors contributing to the epidemic is also important in developing more effective responses. The recommendations draw attention to the importance of rural HIV epidemics and the need to better understand risk and vulnerability in rural contexts in order to effectively respond. Reducing stigma and discrimination directed against people engaging in high-risk behaviors and people living with HIV and AIDS will be critical to support scale up of HIV prevention programs across the countries of the region.

Recommendation 1: Build Capacity

Building capacity to respond to the HIV/AIDS epidemic is a top priority in all South Asia Region countries. This priority component of national AIDS programs includes the following actions:

- building management capacity within government programs at national, state, and local levels

- building nongovernmental organization capacity to work with vulnerable populations and to support and involve community-based organizations in the design and delivery of HIV prevention and care programs

- building capacity at all levels to map vulnerable populations, conduct situation assessments, and analyze and use data generated from these activities.

Recommendation 2: Expand Prevention Programs

All countries in the region must expand prevention programs to saturation level among key subpopulations: female sex workers (SWs) and their clients, injecting drug users (IDUs), men having sex with men (MSM), and male SWs and their clients. These programs must include the following:

- outreach

- peer education

- condom promotion

- provision of sexually transmitted infection treatment and related services

- comprehensive harm reduction for IDUs

- structural interventions at the community level and at higher levels where feasible.

National and external sources must provide the financial, human, and technical resources to support such expansion.

Recommendation 3: Devote Resources to Condom Use and Needle Exchange

Prevention programs need to devote more attention and resources to promoting increased condom use among sex workers, and with both their regular partners as well as their commercial clients. Prevention programs among IDU subpopulations need to devote more attention and resources to comprehensive harm reduction approaches, including needle exchange and drug substitution.

Recommendation 4: Increase and Expand Baseline and Continued Surveillance

HIV surveillance and second-generation integrated bio-behavioral surveillance need to be expanded and further supported in all countries in the region to provide a better understanding of the heterogeneity of the HIV epidemic. Surveillance efforts should in particular be expanded with respect to high-risk groups, such as female and male SWs, IDUs, and MSM, with information collected at the subdistrict level in many areas.

Recommendation 5: Conduct Additional Studies

More information from studies of HIV prevalence and correlates in samples from the general population are needed, both to allow for a better understanding of HIV transmission dynamics and to corroborate data obtained from surveys of prenatal clinic populations. With greater use of antiretroviral therapy in the region, HIV prevalence will increasingly become a less accurate marker for HIV risk, requiring other ways of estimating risk, such as incidence studies or prevalence estimates involving young populations (15 to 19 years). Socioeconomic and behavioral studies to gain a better understanding of the structural dynamics of local networks and how to intervene within them effectively are a priority; more knowledge and understanding of stigma and how to reduce it is also critical.

Recommendation 6: Expand Mapping of High-Risk Populations

Expanded and more comprehensive mapping is required at the district and subdistrict levels for high-risk groups, such as female SWs and their clients, IDUs, MSM, and male SWs. Mapping data will indicate the reach required for prevention programs to boost coverage. Additional focused research is needed to delineate the role of MSM and male SWs in the HIV epidemic and to inform the design of appropriate interventions involving these groups.

Recommendation 7: Improve Understanding of Rural Epidemics

Much more knowledge is needed regarding the course of the HIV epidemic and HIV transmission dynamics in rural areas, particularly in India. These areas particularly need study:

- whether and under what circumstances substantial rural epidemics can be maintained on their own

- the extent to which rural epidemics reflect urban epidemics

- the role of local female SWs and other local risk networks in maintaining rural epidemics.

The importance of rural-based intervention and community-driven programs needs to be better understood. Practical approaches to reducing risk and vulnerability among rural populations also need to be developed, particularly in areas experiencing generalizing epidemics.

Recommendation 8: Reduce Stigma

Stigma reduction through multisectoral approaches is essential to provide a supportive environment for risk reduction and to increase access and use of prevention and care services. This includes analysis, policy development and advocacy to reform legal frameworks, increasing awareness among youth through the education sector, development of work place policies for transport and road workers and other labor forces at risk, and information and communications efforts aimed at the general pubic and policy makers at all levels. Increasing the reach of prevention and care programs to vulnerable and often marginalized populations requires the involvement of social sectors, and should be integral to social development and social protection efforts.

Recommendation 9: Improve Coordination by Expanding Cooperation

Some of the major challenges in South Asia require regional and cross-border programmatic cooperation. For example, harm reduction programs in Afghanistan and Pakistan benefit from coordination with similar initiatives in Iran and Central Asia. Coordinated efforts with India, with a focus on migration and SW trafficking, especially to Mumbai, could enhance HIV prevention among SWs in Nepal. The cross-border drug trade and sexual networks between the highest prevalence districts in northeastern India, parts of Bangladesh, and Myanmar underscore the role of migration and call for transregional and intersectoral cooperation. Cooperation and coordination within countries, and across sectors are also important—not only for stigma reduction as discussed above—but to increase access to prevention programs and care programs. It is also important to scale up some of the successful private sector programs for HIV and AIDS prevention and care in the region.

The World Bank Response to AIDS in South Asia

The World Bank has supported efforts to fight HIV and AIDS in South Asia since the first National AIDS Control Project for India in 1992 and has committed US$380 million to support national programs to date. The main components of these projects include surveillance, monitoring and evaluation, targeted interventions for vulnerable subpopulations, blood safety, stigma reduction among the general population, and institutional development for a multisectoral response. Table A.1 summarizes the Bank's HIV/AIDS lending portfolio in South Asia as of 2006.

In November 2005, the South Asia Regional Management team of the World Bank decided to scale up the response to AIDS, drawing on the Bank's comparative advantage, including its convening power across sectors in the following areas:

- mainstreaming a multisectoral response

- conducting strategic economic and sector work

- mobilizing resources to address critical financing gaps

- linking HIV/AIDS to health sector reform

- improving management and financing

- drawing on global knowledge for local adaptation.

A South Asia regional HIV/AIDS team was established to coordinate and support economic sector work, provide technical assistance

Table A.1 World Bank HIV/AIDS Lending Portfolio in South Asia

Country	Project	Amount (US$ millions)[a]	Approval date	Duration
Bangladesh	Health and Population Programme	4/250 (1.6%)	June 30, 1998	1998–2003
	HIV/AIDS Prevention Project	40	Dec. 12, 2000	2001–2007
Bhutan	HIV/AIDS and STI Prevention Project[b]	5.8[c]	June 17, 2004	2004–2009
India	National AIDS Control Project I	84	March 31, 1992	1992–1999
	National AIDS Control Project II	191	June 15, 1999	1999–2006
Pakistan	Social Action Programme II	2/250 (0.8%)	March 24, 1998	1998–2003
	HIV/AIDS Prevention Project	37.11[d]	June 5, 2003	2003–2007
Sri Lanka	Health Services Project	5/18.8 (26.6%)	Dec. 19, 1996	1996–2002
	HIV/AIDS Prevention Project	12.6	Dec. 17, 2002	2002–2006
	Total	381.51		

a. For projects focused on HIV/AIDS, the full commitment amount is displayed. For those with HIV/AIDS-related components, the commitment amounts for the component and whole project are shown.
b. One of four active projects in the World Bank's Bhutan portfolio and the only health-related project to date.
c. 100 percent grant.
d. 25 percent grant.

and build capacity, and foster internal and external partnerships and communication. Following are some of the activities:

• assessment of the socioeconomic impact of the HIV/AIDS epidemic and a costing study of antiretroviral therapy (India)

• institutional analysis (Nepal)

• HIV/AIDS mapping and assessment of groups at high risk (Afghanistan)

• intercountry consultations on injecting drug use and AIDS and on school health

• development of private sector and workplace programs.

Definition of Targeted and General Population Interventions

Table B.1 provides examples of focused or targeted HIV prevention interventions. These are evidence-based preventive intervention packages, tailored specifically for groups such as youth, women, injecting drug users, men having sex with men, migrants, and employed workers. Included are also other high impact interventions that can be aimed at the general population, such as condom promotion, blood safety, reproductive health services, and services for management of sexually transmitted infections.

For each intervention, the core services are listed and suggested indicators provided for measuring the outcomes of the interventions, or proxies for outcomes. The table also provides a list of opportunities for convergence of programs and integration of services to expand coverage. Treatment and care interventions are not included in this list, other than reproductive tract infection/STI case management, and harm reduction services.

Table B.1 Examples of HIV Prevention Interventions

Prevention intervention	Core services	Outcome (proxy) indicator	Opportunities to expand coverage
Reproductive tract infection and sexually transmitted infection (STI) case management	Syndromic management; single-shot options	Percentage of STI cases assessed and treated; percentage advised on correct and consistent condom use; percent whose partners received treatment	Convergence with reproductive health programs; integration into rural health and private sector programs
Condom promotion	Promotion of knowledge and consistent use, including peer education; increased access	Percentage of correct and consistent condom use in different subpopulations	Health services; peer education; strategic communication; transportation; rural development; private sector
Comprehensive harm reduction interventions for IDUs	Peer education; needle and syringe exchange; oral substitution; residential care; drug de-addiction; health service referrals	HIV prevalence among IDUs	Peer education; community-driven and nongovernmental organization (NGO)–delivered services; strategic communication; legal reform; law enforcement sensitization
Services for men having sex with men (MSM)	Peer education; condom and lubricant supplies; community-based response and risk reduction services; STI service referrals	HIV prevalence among MSM	Peer education; community-driven and NGO-delivered services; strategic communication; legal reform; law enforcement sensitization
Workplace interventions	Workplace policies, protocols, and activities (for example, HIV/AIDS code; information, education, and communication; voluntary counseling and testing referrals)	Percentage of employees with access to HIV/AIDS information and services	Private sector, including firms, trade groups, and labor unions

(continued)

Table B.1 Examples of HIV Prevention Interventions *(continued)*

Prevention intervention	Core services	Outcome (proxy) indicator	Opportunities to expand coverage
Blood safety	Voluntary blood donation; HIV screening of blood units; rational use of blood; quality assurance of blood banks	HIV incidence of bloodborne viral infection	Health services; international blood banking organizations, such as Red Cross or Red Crescent health systems
Youth-friendly services	Life skills training on sexuality and substance abuse; comprehensive health, educational, and social services, including peer education	HIV prevalence among adolescents	Education; athletic leagues; community-driven and social development schemes
Migrant support center	Peer education for behavioral change; health service referrals	HIV prevalence among migrants	Transportation services; social development and services
Female HIV prevention	Health service referrals; community-based responses	HIV prevalence among prenatal clinic population	Convergence with reproductive health programs; integration into rural health and private sector programs

Country Analysis Summaries

Table C.1 summarizes the situational analysis for countries in the South Asia Region, including epidemic potential, epidemic phase, special considerations, and specific recommendations.

Table C.1 Summary of HIV Epidemic Dynamics and Program Recommendations

Factor	India	Nepal	Pakistan	Bangladesh	Sri Lanka	Afghanistan	Rest of South Asia
Epidemic potential	Local concentrated epidemics are widespread, with substantial connections attributable to mobility. Concentrated epidemics are more densely distributed in parts of the southern states, especially Andhra Pradesh, Karnataka, Maharashtra, and Tamil Nadu. Female sex work is central to transmission dynamics in most locations. Men having sex with men (MSM) probably more important than previously assessed. Injecting drug users (IDUs) drive the epidemics in the northeastern states and IDU-linked epidemics are present in some large urban centers.	The potential exists for substantial concentrated epidemics, mostly related to commercial sex and IDU networks. Migration and trafficking of SWs, especially to Mumbai, is amplifying the local epidemic and making it more difficult to control.	High potential exists for local concentrated epidemics in major urban areas (such as Karachi, Lahore, and Multan). Major focuses are likely to be IDUs, female SWs and their clients, and MSM. IDU and MSM epidemics are likely to quickly become linked with sex work, amplifying the local epidemics. Low potential exists for a generalizing epidemic in any of the locations. Lack of information on sexual behaviors and networks in rural areas precludes an assessment of epidemic potential there.	Potential exists for substantial concentrated epidemics, mostly in relation to commercial sex networks. The common and relatively rapid transition from smoking drugs to injecting drugs is disturbing. Evidence of growing HIV infection among IDUs underscores the urgency of harm reduction. Linked epidemics (among female SWs and their clients, IDUs, and MSM) could expand the overall epidemic more quickly.	Better economic and social indicators and low prevalence to date suggest limited epidemic potential.	Epidemic potential is high among IDUs and unknown among MSM.	Epidemic potential is low in the Maldives and in Bhutan.

(continued)

Table C.1 *(continued)*

Factor	India	Nepal	Pakistan	Bangladesh	Sri Lanka	Afghanistan	Rest of South Asia
Epidemic potential *(continued)*	High levels of sexually transmitted infections (STIs), especially among sex workers (SWs) and their clients may exacerbate transmission potential. The potential for a generalizing epidemic exists in some high-prevalence districts, notably in southern India. More data are needed for northern states. The epidemic in much of northern India and other rural areas likely depends on out-migrants who are epidemiological bridges to migration origins. Epidemic potential depends on the size and extent of local high-risk populations.							

(continued)

Table C.1 *(continued)*

Factor	India	Nepal	Pakistan	Bangladesh	Sri Lanka	Afghanistan	Rest of South Asia
Epidemic phase	Although data suggest the epidemic might have reached a plateau in some areas of southern India, epidemics are still incipient or in the early growth phase in many rural districts of southern India. Not enough information is available to characterize the epidemic phase fully in many areas, especially in northern India.	The epidemic is more advanced among some female SW groups and clients than in other countries of the region.	An IDU epidemic appears to be in the growth phase in Sindh province and perhaps elsewhere. An incipient epidemic is associated with female SWs and likely with MSM. High levels of male circumcision may curtail substantial heterosexual epidemics.	The country remains in a relatively early epidemic phase, except among IDUs, where the potential for substantial and rapid epidemic growth exists. High levels of male circumcision may curtail substantial heterosexual epidemics.	The country remains in an early epidemic phase.	The epidemic among IDUs and their partners could escalate rapidly unless quick investment and action are undertaken.	Epidemics in Bhutan and the Maldives are in an early phase and are fueled by migrants and travelers.
Special issues	MSM transmission dynamics are probably more important than previously judged. Mobility of SWs and clients is important for linking local concentrated epidemics.	Female SW migration to India is important. Civil unrest could further displace the population and might increase the supply and demand for sex work.	The linkage of female SWs, IDUs, and MSM could result in explosive epidemic growth in these groups. Dispersion of sex work will make programming difficult but could slow epidemic growth.	A window of opportunity exists for truncating the epidemic through saturation coverage of targeted interventions in high-risk groups.	In a low-prevalence epidemic such as Sri Lanka's, secondary prevention, including working intensively with those already infected to provide treatment and support, is commensurately more important than elsewhere in the region.	Injecting drug use is high in Afghanistan, which is the world's largest heroin producer and exporter and a significant consumer of opium and heroin.	In Bhutan, cross-border programmatic cooperation is vital.

(continued)

Table C.1 (continued)

Factor	India	Nepal	Pakistan	Bangladesh	Sri Lanka	Afghanistan	Rest of South Asia
Recommendations	Expand mapping and situation assessments across northern India and in rural areas of southern India. Rapidly scale up focused prevention programs and targeted interventions to achieve saturation coverage of large and small urban areas (female SWs, their clients and partners, MSM, and IDUs). Develop and quickly implement a rural prevention strategy, with an emphasis on focused prevention programs among high-risk sexual networks. Strengthen capacities for implementing targeted interventions through training and supportive supervision. Create an enabling environment for targeted interventions through multisector involvement in stigma reduction, information and education, legal framework, private sector engagement.	Rapidly scale up focused prevention programs and targeted interventions for female SWs, their clients, and partners, as well as MSM and IDU, where populations at risk are identified. Develop special programming for migrant SWs. Concentrate efforts along the main highways. Strengthen capacities for implementing targeted interventions through training and supportive supervision. Multisector involvement in information, education, and communication; legal framework; stigma reduction; and outreach.	Rapidly scale up focused prevention programs and targeted interventions and services for IDUs, female SWs, their clients, and MSM. Expand mapping and assessments of transmission dynamics in diverse populations to elucidate the epidemic potential. Strengthen capacities for implementing targeted interventions through training and supportive supervision. Create an enabling environment for targeted interventions through multisector involvement in stigma reduction, information and education, legal framework.	Complete a comprehensive mapping of high-risk locations in both urban and rural areas. Rapidly scale up IDU interventions, as the first priority, and expand female SW and MSM interventions. Strengthen capacities for implementing targeted interventions through training and supportive supervision. Create an enabling environment for targeted interventions through multisector involvement in stigma reduction, information and education, legal framework.	Increase coverage of prevention programs for male and female SWs, their clients, and MSM. Build capacity to monitor and curtail injecting drug use. Create an enabling environment for targeted interventions, through multisector involvement in stigma reduction, information and education, legal framework, private sector engagement.	Prioritize harm reduction among IDUs. Create an enabling environment for targeted interventions, such as harm reduction through multisector involvement in stigma reduction, information and education, legal framework, outreach.	Create an enabling environment for targeted interventions, through multisector involvement in stigma reduction, awareness, information and education.

References

Adrien, A., P. Chatterjee, A. Costigan, D. Singh, K. Singh, and P. Singh. 2005. *HIV/AIDS and Migration in Rajasthan*. Jaipur, India: India-Canada Collaborative HIV/AIDS Project.

Altaf, A., S. A. Shah, and A. Memon. 2003. *Follow-Up Study to Assess and Evaluate Knowledge, Attitudes, and High-Risk Behaviours and Prevalence of HIV, HBV, HCV, and Syphilis among IDUs at Burns Road DIC, Karachi*. Islamabad: United Nations Office for Drug Control and Crime and Joint United Nations Programme on HIV/AIDS.

APAC (AIDS Prevention and Control Project). 2004. "HIV Risk Behavior Surveillance Survey in Tamil Nadu Wave IX-2004." APAC, Chennai, India. http://www.apacvhs.org/Pdf/BSS_tamilnadu.pdf.

———. 2005a. "Prevalence of STI and HIV among Women in Prostitution." APAC, Chennai, India. http://www.apacvhs.org/PDF/womeninprostitution.pdf.

———. 2005b. "Prevalence of STI and HIV among General Population in Tamil Nadu." APAC, Chennai, India. http://www.apacvhs.org/PDF/generalpopulation.pdf.

Auvert, B., D. Taljaard, E. Legarde, J. Sobngwi-Tambekou, R. Sitta, and A. Puren. 2005. "Randomized, Controlled Intervention Trial of Male Circumcision for Reduction of HIV Infection Risk: The ANRS 1265 Trial." *PLoS Medicine* 2 (11): e298.

Baqi, S., S. A. Shah, M. A. Baig, S. A. Mujeeb, and A. Memom. 1999. "Seroprevalence of HIV, HBV, and Syphilis and Associated Risk Behaviors in Male Transvestites (*Hijras*) in Karachi, Pakistan." *International Journal of STD and AIDS* 10: 300–4.

Becker, M. L., Paul S. Reza, B. M. Ramesh, R. Washington, S. Moses, and J. F. Blanchard. 2005. "Association between Medical Injections and HIV Infection in a Community Based Study in India" [Letter]. *AIDS* 19: 1334–36.

Blanchard, J. F., B. M. Ramesh, H. Kang, P. Bhattacharjee, R. Washington, and S. Moses. 2005. "Variability in the Sexual Structure of Rural Populations in India: A Case Study." Paper prepared for the 15th Biennial Congress of the International Society for Sexually Transmitted Disease Research, Amsterdam, Netherlands, July 10–13.

Bongaarts, J., P. Reining, P. Way, and F. Conant. 1989. "The Relationship between Male Circumcision and HIV Infection in African Populations." *AIDS* 3: 373–77.

Chao, A., M. Bulterys, F. Musanganire, P. Habimana, P. Nawrocki, E. Taylor, A. Dushimimana, and A. Saah. 1994. "Risk Factors Associated with Prevalent HIV-1 Infection among Pregnant Women in Rwanda." *International Journal of Epidemiology* 23: 371–80.

FHI (Family Health International). 2002. *Rapid Qualitative Study of Female Sex Workers in Pokhara: A Focused Ethnographic Study.* Kathmandu: FHI.

FHI and CREHPA (Family Health International and Centre for Research on Environment, Health and Population Activities). Summary Report 2004. Available: www.fhi.org/en/HIVAIDS/country/Nepal/index.htm.

FHI and NCASC (Family Health International and National Center for AIDS and Sexually Transmitted Disease Control, Government of Nepal, Ministry of Health). 2002. *Injecting and Sexual Behaviors of Male Injecting Drug Users in Pokhara: A Focused Ethnographic Study.* Kathmandu: FHI and NCASC.

FHI, New Era, and SACTS (Family Health International, New Era, and STD/AIDS Counseling and Training Service). 2002a. *HIV Behavioral Surveillance of Female Sex Workers and Male Sub-population Groups in the Midwestern-Eastern Terai Highway Area.* Kathmandu: FHI.

———. 2002b. *Kathmandu Female Sex Worker HIV/STI Prevalence Study.* Kathmandu: FHI.

———. 2003a. *Behavioral and Sero-prevalence Survey among Injecting Drug Users in Eastern Nepal.* Kathmandu: FHI.

———. 2003b. *Behavioral and Sero-prevalence Survey among Male Injecting Drug Users in the Pokhara Valley.* Kathmandu: FHI.

Furber, A. S., J. N. Newell, and M. M. Lubben. 2002. "A Systematic Review of Current Knowledge of HIV Epidemiology and of Sexual Behavior in Nepal." *Tropical Medicine and International Health* 7 (2): 140–48.

Gangopadhyay, D. N., M. Chanda, and K. Sarkar. 2005. "Evaluation of Sexually Transmitted Diseases/Human Immunodeficiency Virus Intervention Programs for Sex Workers in Calcutta, India." *Journal of Sexually Transmitted Infections* 32 (11): 680–84.

Ghauri, A. K., S. A. Shah, and A. Memon. 2003. *Follow-up Study to Evaluate Change in KAPB and Sero-prevalence of HIV, HBV, HCV, and Syphilis among IDUs at DIC, Essa Nagri, Karachi*. Islamabad: UNODC/UNAIDS.

Gibney, L., N. Saquib, M. Macaluso, K. N. Hasan, M. M. Aziz, A. Y. Khan, and P. Choudhury. 2002. "STD in Bangladesh's Trucking Industry: Prevalence and Risk Factors." *Sexually Transmitted Infections* 78 (1): 31–36.

GTZ (German Corporation for Technical Cooperation). 2005. *Integrated Local Drug Prevention, Treatment, and Rehabilitation Project in Afghanistan (IDPA)*. Eschborn, Germany: GTZ/FCO.

Halperin, D. T., and H. Epstein. 2004. "Concurrent Sexual Partnerships Help to Explain Africa's High HIV Prevalence: Implications for Prevention." *Lancet* 363: 4–6.

ICHAP (India-Canada Collaborative HIV/AIDS Project). 2004. *Community-Based HIV Prevalence Study in ICHAP Demonstration Project Area, Key Findings*. Bangalore, India: ICHAP.

Islamic Republic of Afghanistan, Ministry of Public Health DG Preventive Medicine and PHC National HIV/AIDS and STI Control Program. 2006. "Afghanistan National Strategic Plan for HIV/AIDS (2006–2010)." Working Draft.

Khan, M. S. 1996. "KABP Survey on AIDS among *Hijras* in Taxila." Dissertation, Health Services Academy, Islamabad.

KSAPS and ICHAP (Karnataka State AIDS Prevention Society, Government of Karnataka, and India-Canada Collaborative HIV/AIDS Project). 2002. *Karnataka HIV Status Reports: Report on HIV Sentinel Surveillance 2002*. Bangalore, India: KSAPS and ICHAP.

———. 2003. *Karnataka HIV Status Reports: Report on HIV Sentinel Surveillance 2003*. Bangalore, India: KSAPS and ICHAP.

———. 2004. *Karnataka HIV Status Reports: Report on HIV Sentinel Surveillance 2004*. Bangalore, India: KSAPS and ICHAP.

Kumar, R., P. Jha, P. Arora, N. J. Dhingra, and Indian Studies of HIV/AIDS Working Group. 2005. "HIV-1 Trends, Risk Factors, and Growth in India." National Commission on Macroeconomics and Health Background Papers—Burden of Disease in India, Ministry of Health and Family Welfare, New Delhi.

Kumar, R., P. Jha, P. Arora, P. Mony, P. Bhatia, N. Dhingra, M. Bhattacharya, R. S. Remis, N. Nagelkerke. 2006. "Trends in HIV-1 in Young Adults in South India from 2000 to 2004: A Prevalence Study." *Lancet* 367: 1164–72.

Lakshman, M., and M. Nichter. 2000. "Contamination of Medicine Injection Paraphernalia Used by Registered Medical Practitioners in South India: An Ethnographic Study." *Social Science and Medicine* 51: 11–28.

MAP (Monitoring the AIDS Pandemic). 2005. *AIDS in Asia: Face the Facts*. Bangkok: MAP. http://www.mapnetwork.org/reports.shtml.

Mirza, Z., and M. Hasnain. 1995. *KAP Study of Homosexuals about AIDS in Pakistan*. Islamabad: National AIDS Control Programme, Government of Pakistan.

MOPH (Ministry of Public Health, Transitional Islamic Government of Afghanistan). 2003. "HIV/AIDS and STI National Strategic Plan for Afghanistan, 2003–2007" Ministry of Public Health of the Transitional Islamic Government of Afghanistan, Kabul.

Morris, M., and M. Kretzschmar. 1997. "Concurrent Partnerships and the Spread of HIV." *AIDS* 11: 641–48.

NACO (National AIDS Control Organization, Government of India, Ministry of Health and Family Welfare). 2001a. *National Baseline General Population Behavioral Surveillance Survey—2001*. New Delhi: NACO. http://www.nacoonline.org/publication/31.pdf.

———. 2001b. *National Baseline High-Risk and Bridge Population Behavioral Surveillance Survey—2001, Part I (FSWs and Their Clients)*. New Delhi: NACO. http://www.nacoonline.org/publication/41.pdf.

———. 2001c. *National Baseline High-Risk and Bridge Population Behavioral Surveillance Survey—2001, Part II (MSM and IDUs)*. New Delhi: NACO. http://www.nacoonline.org/publication/51.pdf.

———. 2002. *Handbook of Indicators for Monitoring National AIDS Control Programme—II*. New Delhi: NACO. http://www.nacoonline.org/publication/6.pdf.

———. 2005. "An Overview of the Spread and Prevalence of HIV/AIDS in India." NACO, New Delhi. http://www.nacoonline.org/facts_overview.htm.

NACP (National AIDS Control Program, Government of Pakistan, Ministry of Health). 2004. *HIV/AIDS Surveillance Report: October–December 2004*. Islamabad: NACP.

———. 2005a. *Integrated Biological and Behavioural Surveillance: A Pilot Study in Karachi 2004–05*. Islamabad: NACP.

———. 2005b. *National Study of Reproductive Tract and Sexually Transmitted Infections in Pakistan: Survey of High-Risk Groups in Lahore and Karachi*. Islamabad: NACP.

NACP and Naz Foundation International. 2005. *Social Assessment and Mapping of Men Who Have Sex with Men in Lahore, Pakistan*. Islamabad: NACP.

NASP (National AIDS and Sexually Transmitted Disease Programme, Government of Bangladesh, Ministry of Health and Family Welfare, Directorate-General of Health Services). 2004. *HIV in Bangladesh: The Present Scenario: A Summary of Key*

Findings from the Fifth Round of Serological and Behavioral Surveillance for HIV in Bangladesh (2003–2004). Dhaka: NASP.

———. 2005. *National HIV Serological Surveillance, 2004–2005, Bangladesh, Sixth Round Technical Report*. Dhaka: NASP.

NCASC and FHI (National Centre for AIDS and Sexually Transmitted Disease Control, Government of Nepal, Ministry of Health, and Family Health International). 2003. *National Estimates of Adult HIV Infections Nepal 2003*. Kathmandu: NCASC and FHI.

NCHADS, FHI, UCLA, and East-West Center (National Centre for HIV/AIDS, Dermatology and Sexually Transmitted Disease; Family Health International; University of California at Los Angeles; and East-West Center). 2002. *Cambodia Working Group on HIV/AIDS Projection*. Phnom Penh: NCHADS.

NHCPP (National HIV/AIDS Control and Prevention Project). 2005. *Behavioral Surveillance: Terms of Reference*. Colombo: National HIV/AIDS Control and Prevention Project.

NSACP (National Sexually Transmitted Disease and AIDS Control Programme, Government of Sri Lanka, Ministry of Health, Department of Health Services). 2005. *HIV Sentinel Surveillance Survey in Sri Lanka: Report of the 2004 Survey*. Colombo: NSACP.

"Pattern of Drug Abuse prior to Imprisonment among Prisoners Convicted and Remanded for Drug Offences at Welikada Prison." 2003. Dissertation, University of Colombo, Sri Lanka.

Patterson, B. K., A. Landay, J. N. Siegel, Z. Flener, D. Pessis, A. Chaviano, and R. C. Bailey. 2002. "Susceptibility to Human Immunodeficiency Virus-1 Infection of Human Foreskin and Cervical Tissue Grown in Explant Culture." *American Journal of Pathology* 161: 867–73.

Peak, A., S. Rana, S. H. Maharjan, D. Jolley, and N. Crofts. 1995. "Declining Risk for HIV among Injecting Drug Users in Kathmandu, Nepal: The Impact of a Harm-Reduction Programme." *AIDS* 9: 1067–70.

Pike, L. 1999. "Innocence, Danger, and Desire: Representations of Sex Workers in Nepal." *re/productions* 2 (April). http://www.hsph.harvard.edu/grhf/SAsia/.

Policy Project. 2004. *Coverage of Selected Services for HIV/AIDS Prevention, Care, and Support in Low and Middle Income Countries in 2003*. Washington, DC: Policy Project. http://www.futuresgroup.com/Documents/CoverageSurveyReport.pdf.

Quinn, T. C., M. J. Wawer, N. Sewankambo, D. Serwadda, C. Li, F. Wabwire-Mangen, M. O. Meehan, T. Lutalo, and R. H. Gray. 2000. "Viral Load and Heterosexual Transmission of Human Immunodeficiency Virus Type 1: Rakai Project Study Group." *New England Journal of Medicine* 342: 921–29.

Reid, G., and G. Costigan. 2002. *Revisiting "the Hidden Epidemic": A Situation Assessment of Drug Use in Asia in the Context of HIV/AIDS.* Melbourne: Centre for Harm Reduction, Burnet Institute.

Reynolds, S. J., M. E. Shepherd, A. R. Risbud, R. R. Gangakhedkar, R. S. Brookmeyer, A. D. Divekar, S. M. Mehendale, and R. C. Bollinger. 2004. "Male Circumcision and Risk of HIV-1 and Other Sexually Transmitted Infections in India." *Lancet* 363: 1039–40.

Reza Paul, S., S. Moses, B. M. Ramesh, S. Halli, R. Washington, S. Modal, and J. F. Blanchard. 2005. "An Integrated Behavioral and Biological Study among Female Sex Workers in Mysore, India [Abstract MP-106]." Paper prepared for the 15th Biennial Congress of the International Society for Sexually Transmitted Disease Research (ISSTDR), Amsterdam, Netherlands, July 10–13.

Saravanapavananthan, P. T. 2002. "Estimation of Human Immunodeficiency Virus Infections Utilizing the Sexual Behavioral Pattern among Selected High Vulnerable Groups in Colombo District and the Explanation for the Gap between Reported and Estimated Cases in Sri Lanka." Dissertation, University of Colombo, Sri Lanka.

Swasti and KHPT (Karnataka Health Promotion Trust). 2004. *Mapping High Risk Activities in Karnataka.* Bangalore: Swasti and KHPT.

Szabo, R., and R. V. Short. 2000. "How Does Male Circumcision Protect against HIV Transmission of Human Immunodeficiency Virus Type 1." *New England Journal of Medicine* 342: 921–29.

Tasnim, A., N. Hussein, and R. Kelly. 2005. "Effectiveness of Harm Reduction Programmes for Injecting Drug Users in Dhaka City." *Harm Reduction Journal* 2: 22. http://www.harmreductionjournal.com/content/2/1/22.

UNAIDS (Joint United Nations Programme on HIV/AIDS). 2002. "Sex Work and HIV/AIDS: A Technical Update." UNAIDS, Geneva.

———. 2004. *Report on the Global AIDS Epidemic—Fourth Global Report.* Geneva: UNAIDS.

UNICEF and NACP (United Nations Children's Education Fund and National AIDS Control Programme, Government of Pakistan, Ministry of Health). 2002. *A Behavioral Mapping Study of FSWs in Lahore, Karachi, and Multan.* Islamabad: Technical Alliance for Social Change.

UNODC (United Nations Office on Drug Control and Crime). 2002. *Drug Abuse in Pakistan: Results from the Year 2000 National Assessment.* New York: United Nations.

———. 2004. *World Drug Report 2004 of the UNODC.* Vienna: UNODC. http://www.unodc.org/unodc/en/world_drug_report_2004.html.

————. 2005a. *Afghanistan Drug Use Survey 2005*. Vienna: UNODC and Afghanistan Ministry of Counter Narcotics. http://www.unodc.org/pdf/afg/2005Afghanistan DrugUseSurvey.pdf.

————. 2005b. *World Drug Report 2005*. Vienna: UNODC. http://www.unodc.org/ unodc/world_drug_report.html.

U.S. Bureau of the Census. 2006. The HIV/AIDS Surveillance Data Base. Health Studies Branch, International Programs Center, Population Division, U.S. Bureau of the Census, Washington, DC. http://www.census.gov/ipc/www/ hivaidsn.html.

Weiss, H., M. Quigley, and R. Hayes. 2000. "Male Circumcision and Risk of HIV Infection in Sub-Saharan Africa: A Systematic Review and Meta-analysis. *AIDS* 14: 2361–70.

Zafar, T., H. Brahmbhatt, G. Imam, S. ul Hassan, and S. A. Strathdee. 2003. "HIV Knowledge and Risk Behaviors among Pakistani and Afghani Drug Users in Quetta, Pakistan." *Journal of Acquired Immune Deficiency Syndromes* 32 (4): 394–98.

Index

Centre for Research on Environment,
  Health and Population
  Activities (CREHPA, Nepal), 28
Ceylon Tourist Board, 72
civil unrest, 98*t*
Committee of Secretaries (Sri Lanka), 72
concurrent partnerships, 13
condom use
  by female sex workers, 21–23
    clients of, 23–24
  by general population, 27
  by injecting drug users having risky
    sex, 30
  by men having sex with men, 25–26
  promotion programs for, 84–85
cost effectiveness of prevention
  programs, xix–xx
cross-border cooperation, 87, 98*t*

drug production areas and injecting drug
  users, 3, 14, 14*f*, 74, 98*t*

Enhanced HIV Control Program
  (Pakistan), 67
epidemic. *See also specific countries*
  central features of Asian epidemic, 3–4
  generalizing, 10–11, 10*f*
  local concentrated, 9–10, 9*f*
  nature of, 1, 2
  phase of, 11, 12*f*, 98*t*
  potential, 7–11, 96–97*t*
  rates. *See specific countries*
  responses to, 10. *See also specific countries*
  truncated, 8–9, 8*f*
Expended UN Theme Group, 62–63

Family Health International (FHI,
  Nepal), 28
Federal Committee on AIDS (Pakistan),
  66
female HIV prevention, 93*t*
female sex workers, 21–23. *See also*
    specific countries
  clients of, 23–24, 29–30, 53, 96*t*,
    98–99*t*
  injecting drug users and, 29–30
  mobility of, 53
  prevalence and spread among, 31–32

general population
  behavioral surveillance and, 26–27
  high-risk male groups in, 35–36, 36*f*
  interventions, 91–93*t*
  prevalence and spread in, 36–39,
    37*f*, 38*f*
generalizing epidemics, 10–11, 10*f*
Global Fund to Fight AIDS,
  Tuberculosis, and Malaria
  (GFATM), 62, 63, 64–65*b*

Health and Population Sector
  Programme (Bangladesh), 69
Health Services Development Project
  (Sri Lanka), 74
heroin users. *See injecting drug users*
heterogeneity of region, xviii
  India case study (Bagalkot District),
    44–50, 46–49*f*
HIV/AIDS and STI Prevention and
  Control Project (Bhutan), 19
homosexual behavior. *See men having
  sex with men (MSM)*

IDUs. *See injecting drug users*
India
  antiretroviral therapy (ART) in, 54, 90
  Bagalkot District case study, 44–50, 46*f*
    HIV epidemiology, 46–47, 47*f*
    sexual structure, 47–50, 48–49*t*
  critical gaps in, 58–59
  cross-border cooperation in, 87
  declining prevalence in South, but
    not North, 51*b*
  drug-producing areas in, 14
  enabling environment in, 56, 99*t*
  epidemic in, xviii, 41–60
    analysis of, 50–53
    overview, 41–44, 42–45*f*
    phase, 98*t*
    potential, 96–97*t*
  female sex workers in, 21–22, 30,
    31–32, 60, 96*t*, 99*t*
    clients of, 23, 24, 99*t*
  general population
    behavioral surveillance in, 26–27
    prevalence and spread in, 36–39,
      37*f*, 38*f*

Mission College Library

18.00

ECO-AUDIT
ENVIRONMENTAL BENEFITS STATEMENT

The World Bank is committed to preserving endangered forests and natural resources. We have chosen to print *India's Undernourished Children: A Call for Reform and Action* on recycled paper with 30 percent post-consumer fiber. The World Bank has formally agreed to follow the recommended standards for paper usage set by the Green Press Initiative, a nonprofit program supporting publishers in using fiber that is not sourced from endangered forests. For more information, visit www.greenpressinitiative.org.

The printing of these books on recycled paper saved the following:

- 5 trees (40' in height. 6–8 inches in diameter)

- 269 pounds of solid waste

- 2,345 gallons of water

- 508 pounds of net greenhouse gases

- 3.9 million BTUs of total energy

Received

DEC 1 3 2011

Mission College Library